MAKE OUTSTANDING THINGS HAPPEN WITH CENTER OF EXCELLENCE

MOTIVATION   LEADERSHIP SUCCESS

AJAYA GUPTA

The publication of this book is designed to help the individuals to know their potentials and succeed in their life. Since the individual success is tailored to his or her own circumstances, hence there is no guarantee for success. The reader of this publication assumes his or her responsibility for the use of the information. The author and the publisher assumes no responsibility and or liability whatsoever on behalf of the reader of this publication as the individual's circumstances may differ. For this reason, the individual is advised to consult his or her own advisor regarding the individual's specific situation.

Author has taken reasonable precautions in preparation of this book and believes that the facts presented are accurate as of the date when the book was written. However the author and the publisher do not take any liability whatsoever for any name, character, diagrams or any information used in this publication. Neither the author nor the publisher assumes any responsibility for any errors, inaccuracies or omissions. The author and publisher specifically disclaim any liability resulting from the use of application of the information contained in this book, and the is not intended to serve as legal, financial, or other professional advise related to individual specific situation.

Published and designed by CreateSpace, an Amazon company

Dedications

I dedicate this book in loving memory of my Parents, who held very high values of excellence, integrity and purity of thought and character.

"One of the greatest gifts I ever got from God; was my mom and dad".

My father Prof Dr. Rajendra Gupta was a Medical Professional who was richly qualified with MBBS, DMRE, DMRT (UK), PhD, served the humanity with high integrity and extraordinary distinctions. He led research in Radiology and Cancer Isotopes in the UK and India, and his work/research papers were published extensively. My mother, Sudha Gupta was also highly qualified with a MA, MLitt, and taught Yoga, Sanskrit and Hindi. She was multi-talented, a creative writer and author of several books on Hindu religion. She created a series of Bhajan malas (collection of devotional songs), that always ring soulfully in my ears. She had immense knowledge of scriptures and provided spiritual guidance, which has been awe inspiring and has encouraged me to do well, trust in God and be a good person. She worked closely with Mother Teresa, Nobel Laureate and served the humanity.

My parents encouraged me to achieve high excellences in life, make outstanding things happen, and serve the humanity.

"I deeply pay respects to my wonderful parents,
Who gave me unconditional love
and unwavering support,
as next to God"

CONTENTS

Acknowledgements

I sincerely thank many people who have inspired me to write this book, and they deserve my special commendations.

My wife Tanuja, for her continued love and support, my daughter Dr. Tripti Gupta, a Bio Medical Engineering and Medical graduate who is par exemplary and an author of two books; *The Wonderland of Poetry* and *Emotions Explored,* and my son Anshal Gupta, a Berkeley Scholar and an author of the book; *Elements of Essence.* Their books have been translated into many languages and circulated worldwide.

My sister, Dr. Kiran Agarwal and my brother, Dr. Abhaya Gupta have *authored several Medical books and published Research papers worldwide*. My Father in-law Dr. NK Gami, an eminent cardiologist, authored *7 Medical books* and attained eminence both in UK and India.

I thank Tom Smith, *who wrote the Foreword to this book*, for his eminence, as Executive Coach and incredible leadership, and Sue Sramek to make the book this book indispensable to an ardent reader.

Above all, I thank all my teachers who taught and inspired me for high excellences, and to have a life full of passion, success and fortitude.

> *"Thanks a lot to all, for inspiration and guidance,*
> *As this wonderful publication,*
> *is a source of pure joy*
> *in my life".*

Foreword

It is an honor to participate in the introduction of this book, as it's topic is the foundation of my core beliefs and it's author is a person I admire and hold in high esteem. Ajaya and I met last year when we were brought together with a couple other professionals to work on a rather important and exciting consulting assignment. We came from a different industries and areas of discipline and my expertise for the last 28 years is helping people "market themselves" when it comes to finding the "right fit" jobs. That process, in most ways, is identical to marketing any product.

The assignment required us to work very closely together and allowed me the opportunity to get to know this man quite well and I have seen behind his curtain. That's when I have learned, and continue to learn, that not only does he have a burning desire to help others reach their truest potential for excellence.. it is truly in his DNA and he cannot help himself. I mean "in his DNA" literately, since his mother used to work very closely with Mother Theresa and taught Ajaya well in all aspects of life especially in helping others. That is why he wrote this book, not money and fame.. his reward is intrinsic and eternal.

The premise of this unique book is a fresh look at the old truism "you are what you think you are", which is powerful when learned and practiced every day, but can often fade quickly if ignored. This is a user's manual on how to get to your "Center of Excellence" and keep the positive power turned on and enjoy a loving and fulfilling life. It is not that difficult to accomplish and it is not that difficult to let it fade. I know because it happened to me. Forty-five years ago I started going to several seminars and devouring all the self-improvement books you can imagine by all the big names you know. I totally bought into the concept that I could control my subconscious mind and I proved it to be true. Just like the book said, I began accomplishing all of my career goals, winning cars, trips, cash and even a trophy presented by Zig Zigler and met Tony Robbins. Many contests were won close to the end or even on the last day of the contest, but I remember always truly having a belief that I could pull it off. And when I did win I was happy but not surprised.. I expected it. Then over the years I started taking things for granted and gradually stopped "practicing". I paid a price for the lapse and for some reason found it hard to get back to the top until I regained a fresh perspective on how to teach this old dog renewed tricks. And since school is never out, Ajaya's book will always be in my frequent reference stack.

Ajaya's desire is to take you on his special journey up to the "top", or for many of us.. get back up to the "top". His "Journey of Positive Learning" is an easy and enjoyable trip and his "map" will show you an embraceable process to keep you focused in a simple, personal way that makes you feel comfortable and genuinely in control. The beginning of the book is where you get a chance to get a fresh examination of your personality profile and see what makes you tick today, and what might need some adjusting and..how can you adjust it if you do not know what needs adjusting? Basically, here is where you will gain a great deal of product knowledge and get to know yourself better. It is a great step forward to create your realistic goals. Sometimes you are too close to the subject to be objective.

From there you will learn how to harness the tremendous power of your subconscious mind ... which is where 90% of your brainpower is derived. Think about that for a minute. It is your brain and you will take great pleasure in learning how to be a gentle "control freak" plugging into that power. That combined with proper visualization... can be unstoppable. Learning how to use the art of "lateral thinking techniques" to realistically expand your possibilities is easier than it sounds and can actually be fun. You are also going to get a big dose of how happiness and Karma go hand in hand and how to actually incorporate both into your daily life... don't just give it lip service. While learning many new ways to solve difficult problems, you will also learn how to find and even create real opportunities... yes create your own. The possibilities are endless.

Ajaya ends his book with a look into the future regarding the role Center of Excellence is starting to play today in the Business Intelligence Community. I have a feeling that will be a proverbial game changer and it does not surprise me that he is there on the ground floor. Enjoy!

Tom Smith
Executive Coach/Career Facilitator

EXCELLENCE IS NEVER AN ACCIDENT

"Excellence is never an accident.
It is always the result of
high intention, sincere efforts, and intelligent execution;

It represents
The Wise Choice of many alternatives,

Choice not chance,
Determines
Your destiny"

— Aristotle

Introduction

Though a human mind is capable of doing anything, unfathomed and unimagined before, but at our Individual level we may not be even aware about our own abilities, intelligence, strengths and weakness.

Life isn't about finding yourself. Life is about creating yourself (George B Shaw)

We all have many dark areas of abilities and talents; that are hidden and we may need to really explore them to attain our full potential!

Life is 10% what happens to you and 90% how you react to it (Charles R. Swindoll)

Hence, it is imperative that we may need to be aware of our Synergies, our Abilities/our Halo, Values and Beliefs, our Personality, Potentials, Motivations, Positive Attitude in Life, Imaginations, Creativity, Intelligence and empowerment of our Subconscious Mind, our Happiness, Karma /our actions, which can lead us to the Road for Success in **Making Outstanding Things Happen** in our life, by following the path of **Center of Excellence.**

The quality of a person's life is in direct proportion to his commitment to excellence, regardless of their chosen field of endeavor (Vince Lombardi)

There is lot to learn, to get better and become more successful in our life.

Napoleon Bonaparte, the first emperor of France, and one of the greatest military leaders said "The word impossible is in the dictionary of fools".

We can make many things possible. It's an attitude. Nothing is impossible!

Our Mind vs Zeal for Excellence

The world's greatest accomplishments in Track and Field by the fastest man on the Planet, shows exponential decay of the world records by Usain Bolt setting - 7 World Records in 100m (9.72, 9.69, 9.58), 200m (19.30, 19.19), 4x100m relay (37.10), giving an expression that human beings are capable of achieving anything (anything by definition of odds thought otherwise) which was once termed Impossible, overcome odds with their Energy, Attitude, Mind Empowerment and the Power of Excellence.

Jamaican Usain Bolt became an Olympic legend and called "Lightning bolt–the fastest man alive" for smashing world records and winning 9 gold medals, as a reigning champion at the 2008, 2012 and 2016 Summer Games. In his biography he wrote" *I am trying to be one of the greatest, to be among [Muhammad] Ali and Pele. I have made the sport exciting; I have made people want to see the sport. I have put the sport on a different level*".

It's sheer Zeal for Excellence, Positive Attitude and, raising his Performance to such a level, that the world will always laud him and appreciate his excellence for times to come. He is a phenomenon of the Research for Center of Excellence and a Living Legend of our times.

Being Human is a lucky gift: We get it after 8.4 million cycles of life & death

According to Vedas, the Holy book of Hindus, it mentions that there are 8.4 million cycles of life and death through the living organisms, where the soul transforms before we are born as humans. So being a human is an extremely rare chance to live a life with full Potential. Holy book Bhagavad Gita (verse 2.22) mentions *"Just as one gives up an old shirt to put on a new one, the soul gives up an old body to acquire a new kind of body" (vasāmsi jirnāni yathā vihāya).*

The late scientist, Carl Sagan, in his book Cosmos asserts that *The Dance of Nataraja (Tandava) signifies the cycle of evolution and destruction of the cosmic universe (Big Bang Theory).* He said that *the Hindu religion is the only one of the world's great faiths dedicated to the idea that the Cosmos itself undergoes an immense transformation, and our life said to have 8.4 million cycles of death and rebirths. It is the only religion in which time scales correspond to those of modern scientific cosmology.*

This makes us think that, if we are blessed to be born after so many cycles of life and death, why not make the best out of it, correct!

Everyone has unique Personality and when we truly understand the people around us/the ecosystem, we can become successful individuals, entrepreneurs, better employees and friendlier colleagues.

Our Mind has huge positives. We may also need to know great detail on our immense prowess i.e. Creativity, Intelligence and Sub consciousness Powers.

King Solomon also called Jedidiah, didn't ask for wealth, but for Wisdom and God gave it to him. God is the one who gives gifts to men and women, such as Creativity and it is up to us to discover it and then utilize it.

Though we are gifted with an inherent quota of Creativity and Intelligence, we may need to discover it, get to know it and make use of it to our advantage.

Being Creative is not a hobby; it is a way of life (Eve Marks).

There is a process to discover our Creativity and use it. Let's enrich it.

We can use this potential to our ability to generate something novel and useful (Sternberg & Lubart 1999)

Intelligence is our ability to acquire and apply knowledge and skills. It has been defined in many different ways including as one's capacity for logic, learning, understanding, self-awareness, emotional knowledge, planning and problem solving. Technically it is measured as Intelligence Quotient (I.Q).

Creativity and Intelligence are co-related in our life. All individuals have Creativity and Intelligence, but the question is how much do we understand them and utilize them in our everyday life. Let's use this synergy to our advantage. It's fascinating learning.

Our Mind is like an iceberg. 90% of sub consciousness is hidden. We need to understand ourselves better, our true potentials. Learning to access the subconscious and to fully utilize its gifts can help us to "see" in a new way. Beyond our conscious mind and usual senses the veil is lifted, revealing a world of unlimited possibilities. Think of it, it is storage room of everything that is currently not in your conscious mind. This book will help you explore this area.

We also need to understand "What makes us Happy" as Happiness is a state of Mind. It is essential to be Happy. "Being happy doesn't mean that everything is perfect. It means you've decided to look beyond the imperfections."

We also need to discern "Laws of Karma", which govern our life and attitude. Karma is the Sanskrit word for action, the concept of cause and effect.

We may need to discover "our hidden potentials", our hidden treasures and by Center of Excellence path, achieve our True Potentials.

Center of Excellence is not a wishful thinking, but a Virtue of Outstanding Progressive Attitude of our life. Centers of Excellence(COE) is defined as means of efficiently and effectively managing specific tasks or activities, that may vary with rigors of standards and complexity, but all leading to accomplishment of greater Efficiency and Effectiveness.

Center of Excellence is an Attitude for our Success.

When we grow from Child to Adulthood we pass through a learning curve where every individual growth and progress varies, based on his education and guidance. But if we are focused, guided and mentored, we have a better Sense of Direction to do things better, faster and accomplish higher Objectives in life.

This sets a successful person apart, as his Center of Excellence is infused with training and discipline for progressive accomplishment, with well-trained mind and character.

The Center of Excellence in Business is recognized as doing a set of activities extremely well, having Continuous Improvement and Exceeding Clients' Expectations, by Organized Systems and Operations. Let's visit this Powerful Center of Excellence strategy; to achieve the desired business success.

Let's take Control of OUR FUTURE....as Our Success is in OUR HANDS.

"Excellence is an art won by training and habituation.
We do not act rightly because we have virtue or excellence,
But we rather have those because we have acted rightly.
We are what we repeatedly do.
Excellence, then,
is not an act but a habit"
—Aristotle

What this book can do for you

You will find this book as a "Journey of Positive Learning".

The book may take you from an Ordinary person to an Extraordinary person.

It makes an attempt to make you aware about your Halo, and your Personal positives of Personality, Mind and Mental prowess.

> *"No one saves us but ourselves. No one can and no one may.*
> *We ourselves must walk the path"*
> *-Lord Buddha*

As Tom Smith, an eminent Industry leader and Professional Business coach, who wrote the Foreword to this book, mentions that *"This is a user's manual on how to get to your "Center of Excellence" and keep the positive power turned on and enjoy a loving and fulfilling life".*

This book will **Inspire and motivate you** to **Make Outstanding Things Happen**, and **guide you** as to **How to achieve the Center of Excellence**, in 3 simple steps.

3 Simple Steps in this book:

Step 1. This book will help you to "Understand Your Halo "- Values and Beliefs.

This book will help you to understand your Halo the Personality traits, Personality Style and, Powerful Potential of your Sub-Conscious Mind; How to tap into your incredible Subconscious mind which is 90% latent; use a 5 Step process to understand the Power of Creativity; learn, your innovative prowess; use Amazing Powers of Creativity and Lateral Thinking; Learn the Process of Creativity, and a Creativity Hit-list to "Generate Outcomes", and understand Powers of Lateral Thinking to create New Idea and draw its synergy into your life to create massive transformations with your dynamic thinking and actions.

It will also reminds you of your Values and Beliefs and why one should be Happy? in Attaining Happiness: Creating Positive Center of Excellence. The 6 Keys of Happiness, Learn the Treasure of "12 Laws of Karma" that will change your life, which truly enables you to be a better person, with better Values and Beliefs.

We have so much to learn about ourselves, our abilities and our talent.

"To know yourself as the being underneath the thinker, the stillness underneath the mental noise, the love and joy underneath the pain, is freedom, salvation, enlightenment" Eckhart Tolle

The book offers huge positives as getting to know ourselves. You can gain your positive strengths and improve many hidden talents unknown to you before.

Step 2. This book will "Inspire and motivate you to Make Outstanding Things Happen in your life".

You can achieve greatness in life, and can be an Outstanding Individual by Creating Unexpected things and by Making Difficult things Possible. It draws reference to amazing success story of my triumph against all odds to Export Steel for First time in the country against heavy odds. With Strategic Vision and Sense of purpose, you can be successful in Making Outstanding Things Happen.

Do not go where the path may lead, go instead where there is no path and leave a trail (Ralph Waldo Emerson)

You can learn the 5 Step Process to Solve Difficult Problems and the Role of Critical Thinking to Solve Difficult Problems. The book will inspire you to Exceed the Expectations by Raising the Performance Bar in life. You can learn the 3 Steps for Exceeding the Expectations and 4 Step Process to Raise the Bar.

It will encourage you to "Radiate your Persona by sustained individual brilliance", and draws reflections of my story where I was able to create several Niche Industrial Products by synergy of Creativity and Lateral Thinking in a complex and competitive market place; to gain huge competitive advantage. It will motivate you to stand out from the crowd and create a Niche for yourself.

It will provide you guidance as to How to Outperform the Tasks by Creating the Center of Excellence, with 5 Elements that deeply influence our daily lives and Key Factors influencing Performance/Make Outstanding Things Happen and showcases the Center of Excellence set up in a Business framework.

The book draws attention as to How to lead into the 21st Century by Analytics/Business Intelligence COE, which is one of the fastest growing segments of business. Data Analytics or Business Intelligence is estimated to grow 3000 to 5000% per year in next 3 to 5 years. It visualizes greatness by steering B. I Quotient, which is great Value-add in this era of rapid Technology advancement. You will learn about 8 IT 'meta-trends', and 7 Essential components for BI COE. Data Analytics/BI Potentials are unfolded here.

Step 3. This Part will take you to the "5 Steps Roadmap to Implement the Center of Excellence", *both at the Individual level as well as the Business level.*

At the Individual level you can envision the Foundations that support Excellence in Leadership. In the Business Center of Excellence you can take a closer look at the Strategic centralizing expertise in a COE to make an Organization successful.

Take notes and re-read what you need to understand/imbibe learnings.

"Learning is a progressive activity, it enriches life. There is no short cut"

There are several inferences in the book to understand, learn and to do; Take your personality test, know yourself, and make charts to gains better knowledge and understanding of yourself, Know your SWOT Analysis, improve your Persona with Personality, your Strengths, discover your abilities and "Plan your life on positives". Above all "Create your Niche and Stand-out like a shining Star".

This book may Transform your life as a better person, you may evolve yourself.

You can achieve Outstanding Accomplishments in life, if you follow the path of Center of Excellence. It provides you "an attitude to success".

YOU have the Power to Achieve Greatness; to become a Good Leader, attain Excellences. **Take control of YOUR life and Change the world around YOU.**

"Good Luck, Enjoy Reading,
Evolve yourself, Make Outstanding Things Happen, and
May the Power of Excellence be with You"
—Ajaya Gupta

PART ONE

UNDERSTAND

YOUR

HALO:

VALUES & BELIEFS

Chapter 1

What makes you tick – Personality Traits vs Personality Types

Psychologist Gordon Allport was one of the first to study personality traits and created a list of more than 4,000 personality traits. Later he regrouped these traits into three different categories:

Cardinal traits, Central traits, and Secondary traits:

- **Cardinal traits** are those that are so dominant, that they are expressed across situations and various parts of a person's life. This type of trait is considered rare.
- **Central traits** are the core traits that tend to remain relatively stable throughout life. Many trait theories of personality focus on these traits. These traits serve as the "building blocks" of personality.
- **Secondary traits** characteristics are those that emerge in certain situations. These can be inconsistent and may not remain stable over time.

Understanding examples of personality traits is a great way to start your journey into self-discovery.

Remember, if you're up for the challenge or you want to improve, you can make positive changes to your personality.

Types of Personality Traits

However there are about *198 personality traits* and they may not all fit into one category. Broadly personality traits are simply classified as:

- Actions
- Attitudes
- Behaviors
- Positive Personality Traits
- Negative Personality Traits

Some Positive Personality traits:

- Being honest and taking responsibility for your actions are admirable qualities.
- Adaptability and compatibility are great traits and can help you get along with others.
- Drive and determination will help you keep going no matter what.
- Compassion and understanding mean you relate well to others.
- Patience is a virtue and also a good personality trait.
- Courage will help you do what's right in tough situations.
- Loyalty is a good quality to possess, making others trust you.

Here are a few more to consider:

- Adventurous
- Affable
- Conscientious
- Cultured
- Dependable
- Discreet
- Fair
- Fearless
- Observant
- Impartial
- Independent
- Optimistic
- Intelligent
- Keen
- Gregarious
- Persistent
- Capable
- Charming
- Precise
- Confident
- Dutiful
- Encouraging
- Reliable

- Exuberant
- Helpful
- Humble
- Imaginative
- Meticulous
- Trusting
- Valiant

Negative Personality Traits:

- Lazy
- Picky
- Sullen
- Pompous
- Dishonest
- Finicky
- Sarcastic
- Arrogant
- Cowardly
- Sneaky
- Rude
- Quarrelsome
- Impulsive
- Slovenly
- Self-centered
- Boorish
- Surly
- Unfriendly
- Unruly
- Thoughtless
- Stingy
- Bossy
- Vulgar
- Malicious
- Conceited
- Obnoxious

A number of other characteristics, though not necessarily "bad", can also be considered negative personality traits. For example:

- Shyness
- Self-deprecation
- Fear of failure
- Anxiety

Factors that determine the Personality

According to Carl G. Jung's theory of psychological types [Jung, 1971]; people can be characterized by their preference of general attitude which is called Personality type.

Your personality type can be determined by many factors. One way to discover your personality type is to approach it scientifically, by testing yourself and having a psychologist analyze you. A personality test is rather simple. By answering a few questions about your likes and dislikes and where you would like to go in life, a professional can give you a report detailing the type of personality you have.

In psychology, there are *five factors that determine different personality traits*. The five factors **(OCEAN)** are as follows:

- **O**penness: appreciation for a variety of experiences.
- **C**onscientiousness: planning ahead rather than being spontaneous.
- **E**xtraversion: being sociable, energetic and talkative.
- **A**greeableness: being kind, sympathetic and happy to help.
- **N**euroticism: inclined to worry or be vulnerable or temperamental.

Your personality test assesses how much of each of the big five factors you possess. This helps you to gain more insight into your internal experience so you can make sense of your own thoughts and behaviors.

Do I create my Personality?

Everyone has positive and negative traits in personality. Your personality is set by no one but you. It is in the actions you take and the decisions you make, patient person or not; responsible person or not.

You may not be able to change your personality type, but you can change aspects of your personality by taking determined, active steps to become a more balanced person.

Reading a book can expand your horizons and make you a better individual. Just like taking up a hobby is a great way to become a well-rounded individual. Sports can help you learn teamwork, arts and crafts can make you more patient, volunteering can help you become more caring and a more responsible person in the society that you live in.

Can the Personality affect others?

Being positive and upbeat in life can influence everyone around you, and so can negativity. For example, a friendly smile to a stranger can brighten up their day, just as a glare can frighten them and cause their mood to drop. Bear in mind the famous saying "Do unto others as you would have them do to you".

While you may not be able to help it if you are having a bad day, or if you don't like doing a particular task, changing your attitude changes everything. Complaining and sulking will only make time drag when doing an unpleasant job. Thinking about a fun experience, singing a song in your head or even humming can make the job (and you) just a little easier to deal with. Being a more pleasant person helps everyone.

Preference of General Attitude Theory

According to Carl G. Jung's theory of psychological types [Jung, 1971]; people can be characterized by their preference of general attitude:

- Extraverted (E) vs. Introverted (I), their preference of one of the two functions of perception:
- Sensing (S) vs. Intuition (N), and their preference of one of the two functions of judging:
- Thinking (T) vs. Feeling (F)
- Judging (J) vs. Perceiving (P)

The three areas of preferences introduced by Jung are dichotomies (i.e. bipolar dimensions where each pole represents a different preference). Jung also proposed that in a person one of the four functions above is dominant – either a function of perception or a function of judging. Isabel Briggs Myers, a researcher and practitioner of Jung's theory, proposed to see the judging-perceiving relationship as a fourth dichotomy influencing personality type [Briggs Myers, 1980]:

- The first criterion, **Extraversion – Introversion**, signifies the source and direction of a person's energy expression. An extravert's source and direction of energy expression is mainly in the external world, while an introvert has a source of energy mainly in their own internal world.
- The second criterion, **Sensing – Intuition**, represents the method by which someone perceives information. Sensing means that a person mainly believes information he or she receives directly from the external world. Intuition means that a person believes mainly information he or she receives from the internal or imaginative world.
- The third criterion, **Thinking – Feeling**, represents how a person processes information. Thinking means that a person makes a decision mainly through logic. Feeling means that, as a rule, he or she makes a decision based on emotion, i.e. based on what they feel they should do.
- The fourth criterion, **Judging – Perceiving**, reflects how a person implements the information he or she has processed. Judging means that a person organizes all of his life events and, as a rule, sticks to his plans. Perceiving means that he or she is inclined to improvise and explore alternative options.

Determining Personality Types

Many of today's theories of psychological typology are based on the work of Swiss psychiatrist Carl Gustav Jung, who wrote Psychological Types in 1921. He was the founder of analytical psychology, which studies the motivations underlying human behavior.

Your personality type is a detailed classification of the innate characteristics that make you who you are.

There are many different personality types, 16 according to the Myers-Briggs Type Indicator, but it is sometimes difficult to classify a person as a single type.

Myers-Briggs Personality Types Key:

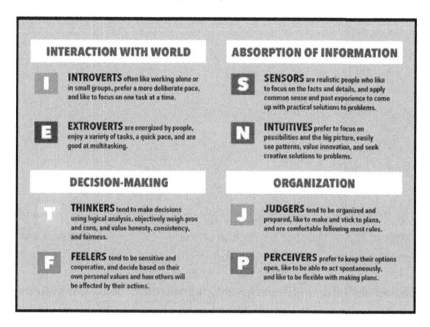

INTERACTION WITH WORLD

I **INTROVERTS** often like working alone or in small groups, prefer a more deliberate pace, and like to focus on one task at a time.

E **EXTROVERTS** are energized by people, enjoy a variety of tasks, a quick pace, and are good at multitasking.

ABSORPTION OF INFORMATION

S **SENSORS** are realistic people who like to focus on the facts and details, and apply common sense and past experience to come up with practical solutions to problems.

N **INTUITIVES** prefer to focus on possibilities and the big picture, easily see patterns, value innovation, and seek creative solutions to problems.

DECISION-MAKING

T **THINKERS** tend to make decisions using logical analysis, objectively weigh pros and cons, and value honesty, consistency, and fairness.

F **FEELERS** tend to be sensitive and cooperative, and decide based on their own personal values and how others will be affected by their actions.

ORGANIZATION

J **JUDGERS** tend to be organized and prepared, like to make and stick to plans, and are comfortable following most rules.

P **PERCEIVERS** prefer to keep their options open, like to be able to act spontaneously, and like to be flexible with making plans.

As with temperament, your type is determined by the strength of your preferences. If, for example, your four dominant preferences are Extraversion (E), Sensing (S), Feeling (F) and Perceiving (P), your personality type would be ESFP. No personality type is better than another. Each person has a unique set of valuable characteristics.

All possible permutations of preferences in the 4 dichotomies above yield 16 different combinations, or personality types, representing which of the two poles in each of the four dichotomies dominates in a person, thus defining 16 different personality types. Each personality type can be assigned a 4 letter acronym of the corresponding combination of preferences:

16 Personality types per Myers-Briggs keys:

- ESTJ
- ISTJ
- ENTJ
- INTJ
- ESTP
- ISTP
- ENTP
- INTP
- ESFJ
- ISFJ
- ENFJ
- INFJ
- ESFP
- ISFP
- ENFP
- INFP

The first letter in the personality type acronym corresponds to the first letter of the preference of general attitude - "E" for extraversion and "I" for introversion.

The second letter in the personality type acronym corresponds to the preference within the sensing-intuition dimension: "S" stands for sensing and "N" stands for intuition.

The third letter in the personality type acronym corresponds to the preference within the thinking-feeling pair: "T" stands for thinking and "F" stands for feeling.

The forth letter in the personality type acronym corresponds to a person's preference within the judging-perceiving pair: "J" for judging and "P" for perception.

For example: ISTJ stands for Introverted, Sensing, Thinking, Judging and ENFP stands for Extraverted, Intuitive, Feeling, and Perceiving.

4 Categories of 16 Personality Types:

Based on temperament they are divided into 4 categories.

SJ Protectors
- ESTJ Overseer
- ESFJ Supporter
- ISTJ Examiner
- ISFJ Defender

SP Creators
- ESTP Persuader
- ESFP Entertainer
- ISTP Craftsman
- ISFP Artist

NT Intellectuals
- ENTJ Chief
- ENTP Originator
- INTJ Strategist
- INTP Engineer

NF Visionaries
- ENFJ Mentor
- ENFP Advocate
- INFJ Confidant
- INFP Dreamer

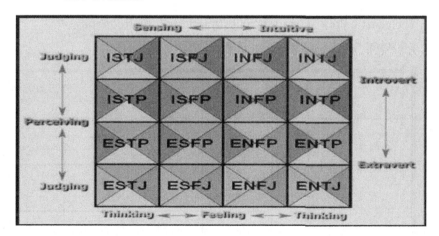

Your personality type includes your preferences, outlook and behavior

- Judging vs Perceiving
- Feeling vs Thinking
- Sensing vs Intuitive
- Extrovert vs Introvert

Understanding your Personality type can be useful in many ways, including relationships, career and school.

What is your Personality? …..Take the personality assessment

There are several free Personality online tests:
- 16personalities; https://www.16personalities.com/
- Jung Typology Test™ http://www.humanmetrics.com/cgi-win/jtypes2.asp
- 14 Free Personality Tests That'll Help You Figure Yourself Out https://www.themuse.com/advice/14-free-personality-tests-thatll-help-you-figure-yourself-out
- Open Source Psychometrics Project https://openpsychometrics.org/

"It's so incredible to finally be understood, who you are and why you do things the way you do"

Personality Types in the Population

The chart below represents an estimation of the frequency of personality types among the population.

TOTAL		ISTJ 11-14%	ISFJ 9-14%	INFJ 1-3%	INTJ 2-4%
E 45-53%	I 47-55%	ISTP 4-6%	ISFP 5-9%	INFP 4-5%	INTP 3-5%
S 66-74%	N 26-34%	ESTP 4-5%	ESFP 4-9%	ENFP 6-8%	ENTP 2-5%
T 40-50%	F 50-60%				
J 54-60%	P 40-46%	ESTJ 8-12%	ESFJ 9-13%	ENFJ 2-5%	ENTJ 2-5%

This chart is just an indicator of Personality type's distribution, but there is lot more to it to understand it and correlate to your type.

What do percentages next to the personality type words or letters mean?

Humanmetrics Jung Typology Test™ (JTT™) and Jung Typology Profiler for Workplace™ (JTPW™) instrument determine the expressiveness of each of the four personality type dimensions (Extraversion vs. Introversion, Sensing vs. Intuition, Thinking vs. Feeling, and Judging vs. Perceiving.)

In JTT™ and JTPW™, the scales of these four dimensions represent a continuum between two opposite poles, from 100 at one pole to 100 at another pole. I.e. Extravert-Introvert dimension is a continuum from 100 on Extraversion (i.e. respondent is a 100% extravert) to 100 on Introversion (i.e. respondent is a 100% introvert). In other words the scale is 200 units long:

Extravert [100% - - - 0% - - - 100%] Introvert

People may reveal features of both poles but typically have a preference of one way over the other. The letter indicates the preference and the percentage indicates the extent of it.

The E-I score of 0% means the respondent is at the borderline between being an extravert and an introvert. Having Extraversion score of greater than 0 - e.g. 20% - means being 20% more slanted toward Extraversion over Introversion. Having Introversion score of greater than 0 - e.g. 20% - means being 20% more slanted toward Introversion over Extraversion.

The same pertains to the S-N, T-F, and J-P dichotomies.

Carl Gustav Jung (1875-1961) Jung called Extraversion-Introversion preference general attitude, since it reflects an individual's attitude toward the external world distinguished by the "direction of general interest" [Jung, 1971]: the extravert maintains affinity for, and sources energy from the outer world, whereas the introvert is the other way around – their general interest is directed toward their inner world, which is the source of their energy.

As mentioned above, Jung introduced a pair of judging functions - thinking and feeling - and a pair of perception functions – sensing (or "sensation"), and intuition.

Sensing-Intuition preference represents the method by which one perceives information: Sensing means an individual mainly relies on concrete, actual information - "in so far as objects release sensations, they matter" [1], whereas Intuition means a person rely upon their conception about things based on their understanding of the world. Thinking-Feeling preference indicates the way an individual processes information. Thinking preference means an individual makes decisions based on logical reasoning; and is less affected by feelings and emotions. Feeling preference means that an individual's base for decisions is mainly feelings and emotions.

Jung introduced the idea of hierarchy and direction of psychological functions. According to Jung, one of the psychological functions - a function from either judging or perception pair – would be primary (also called dominant). In other words, one pole of the poles of the two dichotomies (Sensing-Feeling and Thinking-Feeling) dominates over the rest of the poles. The Extraversion-Introversion preference sets the direction of the dominant function: the direction points to the source of energy that feeds it – i.e. to the outer world for extraverts and to the inner world for introverts.

Jung suggested that a function from the other pair would be secondary (also called auxiliary) but still be "a determining factor" [Jung, 1971] I.e. If Intuition is dominant, then the auxiliary one is either Thinking or Feeling. If Sensing is dominant, then the auxiliary one can also be either Thinking or Feeling. However, if Thinking is dominant, then the auxiliary one is either Sensing or Intuition, and if Feeling is dominant then the auxiliary one is either Sensing or Intuition. In other words, the auxiliary function never belongs to the same dichotomy.

Jung called feeling and thinking types "rational" because they are characterized by the dominance of judging functions that provide reasoning rationale (be it thinking or feeling). "Rational" or Judging preference results in thinking, feelings, response and behavior that consciously operate in line with certain rules, principles or norms. People with dominant "rational" or judging preference perceive the world as an ordered structure that follows a set of rules.

He called sensing and intuitive types "irrational" because they are characterized by dominance of the functions of perception (either sensing or intuition), and therefore their "commissions and omissions are based not upon reasoned judgment but upon the absolute intensity of perception" [Jung, 1971]. "Irrational" or Perceiving preference operates with opportunities, i.e. with a range of possible outcomes that result from assumed premises or from sensations, mostly driven by the unconscious processes.

People with dominant "irrational" or Perceiving preference see the world as a structure that can take various forms and outcomes. It is possible to determine, either by observation or by asking certain questions, preference of Judging vs. Perceiving and the strength thereof in a person.

Traditionally, Personality was determined by Blood Groups:

For several hundred years, humans had Personality determined by Blood Groups for societal disposition, per Japanese and South East Asian countries.

Scientific American mentions that when you bleed, Japan and several South East Asian countries can determine your character by your Blood Group.

When someone acts a certain way, Japanese people like to tease, saying, "Of course you'd do that, you're B," and so on. It facilitates communication and helps people feel more open with one another.

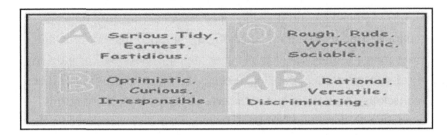

In Japan a person's blood type is popularly believed to determine temperament and personality. "What's your blood type?" is often a key question in everything from matchmaking to job applications.

There are 4 types of Blood Groups: A, B, AB and O: Japanese classified individual characteristics based on blood groups as follows:

- A Personality: Serious, Tidy, Earnest, Fastidious
- B Personality: Optimistic, Curious, Irresponsible
- AB Personality: Rational, Versatile, Discriminating
- Personality: Rough, Rude, Workaholic, Sociable

However, this shows inconsistency of characteristics vs assumed Personality types, as the modern day research is much more scientific and objective.

How to create your Personality Chart on a 20 point scale

This is one of the common ways to understand your attributes

Creating a personality chart is a three Step process.

Step 1: Determine the Personality Traits to Measure.

The first step in creating your personality chart is to determine the personality traits that you're going to measure. I suggest that you measure the following 20 personality traits:

- Charisma – the ability to attract, charm, and influence those around you.
- Perseverance—the ability to keep going despite setbacks and obstacles.
- Confidence – belief in your ability to deal effectively with the world.
- Compassion – sympathy for the suffering of others (or yourself) and wanting to alleviate that suffering.
- Courage – acting despite fear.
- Humor the ability to be amused, and be amusing to others.
- Agreeableness – being kind, approachable, and easy to get along with.
- Resilience – the ability to bounce back from adversity.
- Extraversion – being high energy and sociable.
- Aggression – being forceful and assertive.
- Decisiveness – the ability to make decisions quickly and effectively.
- Integrity – being honest and having strong moral principles.
- Self-Discipline – the ability to stay focused and to do what needs to be done.
- Patience – the ability to tolerate delay, difficulty, or annoyance.
- Curiosity – having a strong desire to learn new things and being open to new experiences.
- Ambition – having a strong desire to achieve.
- Optimism – having the disposition to look at the more favorable side of events, and having the expectation that things will work out well.
- Leadership – the ability to inspire, motivate, and lead other people.
- Conscientiousness – being responsible, having high impulse control, and being dependable.
- Neuroticism – being emotionally unstable and anxious, and having a tendency to overreact.

Step 2. Rate yourself on Each Personality Trait.

Rate yourself on each personality trait on a scale from 1 to 20.

There are three different approaches you can use for this:

- Rate yourself subjectively. Just ask yourself: "How would I rate myself on each of these personality traits?"
- Ask someone you know well to rate you. You can also ask several people for their input and write down the average rating that you receive from them for each of the personality traits.
- Find a test you can use to rate yourself on each of the 20 character traits. For example, here's a test for rating how confident you are.

Step 3: Create your Personality Chart on 20 point scale

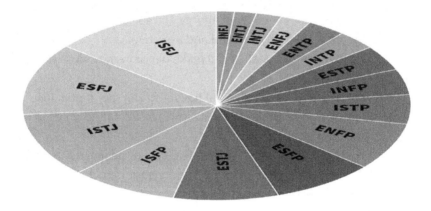

Women vs Men Personality chart will be different on a 20 Point scale

To create your chart, do the following:

- Draw a circle and divide it into 20 segments.
- Label each segment so that each one represents one of the 20 personality traits you're measuring.
- Then, label each spoke of the wheel from 1 to 20, where 1 is closest to the center of the circle, and 20 is the outer edge of the circle.
- For each personality trait, place an "x" on your score or rating for that trait. Lastly, connect all your marks.
- And, there you have it: you've created a personality chart.

After every few months; a 3 to 6 months interval after you've started taking action to modify your personality traits, create another personality chart. How have things changed? Has your score improved for the personality traits you want to change? If not, take corrective action. If so, keep going until you've gotten the results that you're after.

With these steps you can become more resilient, more charismatic (and interesting), and more optimistic. Conduct your own online research, find a book on Amazon, find a self-development course, or attend Training for Motivation, Leadership and Success that will help you to craft a game plan on how to improve and become more dynamic and successful.

After all, it is People skills and we live around people.

"The will to win, the desire to succeed, the urge to reach your full potential... these are the keys that will unlock the door to personal excellence" Confucius

How to Change your Personality

Once you've created your personality chart, then you can analyze it and determine what changes you would like to make.

You can evolve yourself and by continuous improvement, gain strengths in your personality when you know about it.

As an illustration, you may decide that you need to be more resilient and courageous, and that you need to be less aggressive.

Then, create your game plan.

For example, create a post on your 20 Ways to Be More Conscientious, take actions:
- Start reading books where you can learn and improve Attitude.
- Try changing your Temperament and controls Ego and Anger.
- Get more organized, say specify a day, time for paying bills.

- Create a budget and start monitoring your spending habits.
- Start planning your day the evening before.
- Plan your weekly calendar menus: Outline the tasks and develop a game plan of how to accomplish it.
- Organize grocery shopping, and do some prep work so that you can cook and eat healthy meals all week.
- Don't take on more commitments than you can handle.
- Finish what you start.

Understand your Temperament

Temperament is the combination of mental, physical, and emotional traits of a person; natural predisposition, the unusual personal attitude or nature as manifested by peculiarities of feeling, temper, action, etc., often with a disinclination to submit to conventional rules or restraints.

Plot your chart and the indicators on the scale will be matrix of the following indicators to gain an understanding:

- Logical vs Emotional

- Quick vs Slow

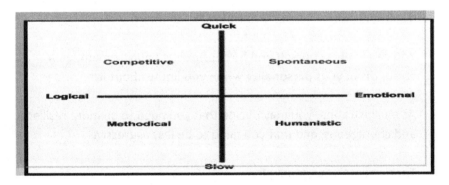

There are several online Temperament tests available but one needs to be careful who is evaluating the results and what are the matrices of examination. It is sensitive as it related to feelings.

You're unique, so is your temperament. *Knowing yourself is very important to grow and improve with Strengths.*

18

Understanding temperament helps in cognitive, academic and social adjustment where we can place groups of individuals together for a team behavior.

There is no personal charm, greater than charm of a cheerful temperament.

"Perfection is not attainable, but if we chase perfection we can catch excellence"- Vince Lombardi.

Develop Excellence: Build Leadership Character

Leaders do not command excellence, they build excellence.

Excellence is "being all you can be" within the bounds of doing what is right for your organization. To reach excellence you must first be a leader of good character. You must do everything you are supposed to do.

"Waste no more time arguing what a good man should be. Be one" - Marcus Aureliu.

Organizations will not achieve excellence by figuring out where it wants to go, having leaders do whatever they have to in order to get the job done, and then hope their leaders act with good character. This type of thinking is backwards.

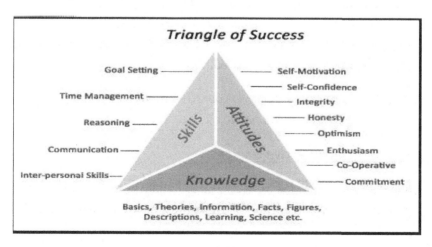

Excellence starts with leaders of good and strong character who engage in the entire process of leadership. And the first process is being a person of honorable character.

Build Excellence in Character

Character develops over time. Many think that much of a person's character is formed early in life. However, we do not know exactly how much or how early character develops. But, it is safe to claim that character does not change quickly. A person's observable behavior is an indication of his or her character. This behavior can be strong or weak, good or bad.

A person with strong character shows drive, energy, determination, self-discipline, willpower, and nerve. They see what they want and go after it. They attract followers.

On the other hand, a person with weak character shows none of these traits. He does not know what he wants. His traits are disorganized; she wavers and is inconsistent. He will attract no followers-Kevin Spacey.

'Live each day as if it is your last. Make your character likeable,' said Mahatma Gandhi. 'Learn as if you'll live forever.'

A strong person can be good or bad. A good leader can set an example, while an outstanding community leader is one with both strong and good characteristics. An organization needs leaders with both strong and good characteristics — people who will guide them to the future and show that they can be trusted.

*"Courage—not complacency—is our need today. Leadership - not salesmanship "*John F. Kennedy.

How to be an Effective Leader

A leader leads from the front and takes initiatives first to set examples for the team to follow. Your followers must have trust in you and they need to be sold on your vision.

Life is 10 percent what you experience and 90 percent how you respond to it.

Korn-Ferry International, an executive search company, performed a survey on what organizations want from their leaders. The respondents said they wanted people who were both ethical and who convey a strong vision of the future. In any organization, a leader's actions set the pace. This behavior wins trust, loyalty, and ensures the organization's continued vitality.

One of the ways to build trust is to display a good sense of character composed of beliefs, values, skills, and traits (U.S. Army Handbook):

- **Beliefs are the things we hold dear to us** and are rooted deeply within us. They could be assumptions or convictions that you hold true regarding people, concepts, or things. They could be the beliefs about life, death, religion, what is good, what is bad, what is human nature, etc.
- **Values are attitudes** about the worth of people, concepts, or things. For example, you might value a good car, home, friendship, personal comfort, or relatives. Values are important as they influence a person's behavior to weigh the importance of alternatives. For example, you might value friends more than privacy, while others might be the opposite.
- **Skills are the knowledge and abilities** that a person gains throughout life. The ability to learn a new skill varies with each individual. Some skills come almost naturally, while others come only by complete devotion to study and practice.

Traits are distinguishing qualities or characteristics of a person, while character is the sum total of these traits.

Let's focus on a few that are crucial for a leader. The more of these you display as a leader, the more your followers will believe and trust in you.

Top 10 Traits of People with Leadership/High Excellences

Per Lolly Daskal President and CEO, Lead from Within, "What you need to find and develop within yourself to be successful? The answer comes from looking at those who have created success in a variety of fields.

These traits may sound simple, but they lead to remarkable results.

1. Drive for Excellence

You have the determination to work harder than most and make sure things get done. You pride yourself on seeing things getting completed and you take charge when necessary. You drive yourself with purpose and align yourself with excellence.

2. Self-reliance

You can shoulder responsibilities and be accountable. You make hard decisions and stand by them. To think for you is to know yourself.

3. Will-power

You have the strength to see things through--you don't vacillate or procrastinate. When you want it, you make it happen. The world's greatest achievers are those who have stayed focused on their goals and been consistent in their efforts.

4. Patience

You are willing to be patient, and you understand that, in everything, there are failures and frustrations. To take them personally would be a detriment.

5. Integrity

It's seriously one of the most important attributes you can cultivate. Honesty is the best policy for everything you do; integrity creates character and defines who you are.

6. Passion

If you want to succeed, if you want to live, it's not politeness but rather passion that will get you there.

7. Connect with others

You can relate to others, which in turns makes everything reach further and deepen in importance.

8. Optimism

You know there is much to achieve and much good in this world and you know what's worth fighting for. Optimism is a strategy for making a better future--unless you believe that the future can be better, you're unlikely to step up and take responsibility for making it so.

9. Self-confidence

You trust yourself. It's as simple as that. And when you have that unshakeable trust in yourself, you're already one step closer to success.

10. Communication

Pay attention to communication. Most important, you hear what isn't being said. When communication is present, trust and respect follow.

No one plans on being mediocre; if you want to succeed, learn the traits that will make you successful, and plan on living them every day.

Be humble and great, courageous and determined, faithful and fearless...your success is in your hands.

> *"Try not to become a man of success,*
>
> *But, Try rather to become a man of value."*
>
> *– Albert Einstein*

Chapter 2

Tap into your Powerful Sub-conscious Mind

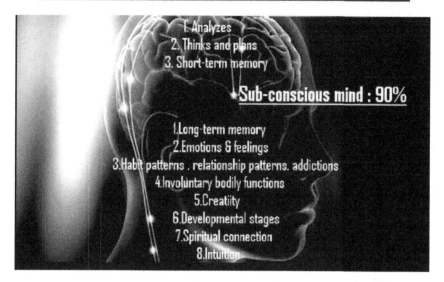

Most of us go about our lives without realizing and utilizing the power of our subconscious minds.

This 90% of our brainpower is derived from the subconscious mind, the part of your brain you are not conscious of. ... In essence, the subconscious mind is the storage room of everything that is currently not in your conscious mind. ... You can manifest ANYTHING YOU WANT AND DESIRE!

Everyday life has some fine examples of our subconscious behavior:

- You haven't logged in to your email account for a long time, and you can't remember your password however hard you think of it... but as soon as you get your hands on the keyboard you type it automatically and voila... the password is accepted....Happens too many times!
- Driving a car is fun; you tend to drive without making a conscious effort to drive, listening to music, observing countryside.

- When you see fire you don't want to touch it no matter under what condition you find yourself. That's subconscious mind in action preventing you from doing that.

"Your subconscious mind controls your behavior and causes you to react rather than respond," states Suze Casey author of Belief Re-patterning: The Amazing Technique for "Flipping the Switch" to Positive Thoughts.

Realizing the Power of your Subconscious mind

Miracles will happen to you, too, when you begin using the magic power of your subconscious mind.

Within your subconscious mind you will find the solution for every problem; and the cause for every effect. Because you can draw out the hidden powers, you come into actual possession of the power and wisdom necessary to move forward in abundance, security, joy, and dominion

"The reason man may become the master of his own destiny is because he has the power to influence his own subconscious mind" Napoleon Hill

Within subconscious depths lies infinite wisdom, infinite power, and an infinite supply of all that is necessary, just waiting for the development and expression.

You should begin now... try to recognize these very potentialities of your deeper mind, and they will take form in the world without.

The infinite intelligence within your subconscious mind can reveal to you, everything you need to know at every moment of time and point of space, provided you are open-minded and receptive.

You can receive new thoughts and ideas enabling you to bring forth new inventions, make new discoveries, or write books and plays. Moreover, the infinite intelligence in your subconscious can impart to you with wonderful kinds of knowledge of an original nature. It can reveal to you and open the way for perfect expression and a true place in your life.

Through the wisdom of your subconscious mind you can attract the ideal companion; as well as the right business associate or partner. It can find the right buyer for your home, and provide you with all the money you need; and the financial freedom to be, to do, and to go, as your heart desires.

"You grow old when you lose interest in life, when you cease to dream, to hunger after new truths, and to search for new worlds to conquer. When your mind is open to new ideas, new interests, and when you raise the curtain and let in the sunshine and inspiration of new truths of life and the universe, you will be young and vital." Joseph Murphy, The Power of Your Subconscious Mind.

Use the power of your conscious and subconscious mind to create a vibrational match for the abundance you desire and deserve." Jack Canfield

Subconscious mind: Your Healthier within

While most of us are aware that we have something called a subconscious mind within us, there are very few of us who know much more than that about it let alone how to harness it.

"If you do not run your subconscious mind yourself, someone else will run it for you." Florence Scovel Shinn

I have seen the power of the subconscious lift people up out of crippled states, making them whole, vital, and strong once more, and free to go out into the world to experience happiness, health, and joy. There is a miraculous healing power in your sub-conscious that can heal the troubled mind and the broken heart.

How to tap into your Subconscious mind: Follow 5 Simple Steps

Step 1. Meditate

Practice Meditation. There are various techniques and Meditation takes you deeper into your consciousness, allowing you to enter a state of being that is akin to dreaming.

In normal life, your brain is normally be functioning in the 'beta' pattern. This state is associated with alertness, but also with stress, anger and anxiety. In meditation, your brain patterns slow and calm down In meditation you move to a higher state where you will notice a change in the quality of your thinking, where random thoughts may seemingly 'pop into your head' but rather the thoughts of your subconscious mind are beginning to assert themselves on your consciousness. That is a great step in the right direction.

Learn to "observe your thought pattern" and they maybe suggest radical, revolutionary solutions to current problems or dilemmas you are facing, it will also be transforming power in your life.

Step 2. Visualize your Goals: Big picture into smaller steps

Think Big! Our brains are excellent at seeing patterns. Dream for a Big Goal in life, something which you want to accomplish. Then start dreaming of smaller steps that it will take to enable you to accomplish the bigger Goal.

Step 3. Definitive Purpose: Objective oriented

The Imagination has to be quantitative, time bound or numeric, something Objective. Say I want to earn 5 million dollars in business by 2020, or get into medical school, or complete so and so task by such and such time. There has to always be a bar to accomplish your goal.

Step 4. Relax and be Confident

Relax, as once you have set a Big Picture and laid the steps, your mind has a journey path to follow.

Be confident that it is you who have set this goal, so something will definitely help you from within to get there.

I use the mantra "everything will happen with perfect timing" and recall times when it was true. For example, one time I was running late for a meeting, but so was the other person.

The best way to get happy and relaxed is to focus on appreciation.

Step 5. Go by your Instincts: Take decisions and get astonishing results

This is a state where your subconscious mind has evolved and at its higher state tells you why you feel this way or why you think it is the 'right' decision. But in actual fact, these decisions that are made in the blink of an eye are usually incredibly perceptive and astonishingly accurate.

Tapping into your creative side can help your subconscious express itself. Many people have reported that practicing art, music, pottery or any other form of self-expression has opened up a side to their personality that they felt was always there but was not being able to be expressed.

Your subconscious mind is always available to you, once you know the way to unlock the door. Once you start living your life in tune with your subconscious you will wonder how you ever got by before – once you are accessing your subconscious mind on a daily basis your life will truly be transformed.

"Act with purpose, courage, confidence, competence and intelligence until these qualities 'lock in' to your subconscious mind." Brian Tracy, *author of 60 books on Psychology and legendary Leadership coach.*

Realize 10 Treasures of your Sub-Conscious Mind

1. The treasure house is within you. Look within for the answer to your Heart's desire.
2. The great secret possessed by the great men of all ages was there to Contact and release the powers of their subconscious mind. You can do the same.
3. Your subconscious has the answer to all problems. When you start driving the car you register so many activities, initially hard but

gradually you drive with ease and subconsciously know when to brake, when to turn and when to stop. It's your inner self evolved.

4. Your subconscious mind is the builder of your mind and can heal you. Lull yourself to sleep every night with the idea of perfect health, and your subconscious, being your faithful servant, will obey you.

5. Every thought is a cause, and every condition is an effect.

6. If you want to write a book, write a wonderful play, give a better talk to your audience, convey the idea lovingly & feelingly to your subconscious mind, and it will respond positively.

7. You are like a captain navigating a ship. He must give the right orders, and likewise, you must give the right orders (thoughts and images) to your subconscious mind, which controls and governs all your Experiences.

8. Never use the terms, "I can't afford it" or "I can't do this." Your subconscious mind takes you at your word and sees to it that you do not have the money or the ability to do what you want to do. Affirm, "I can do all things through the power of my subconscious mind."

9. The law of life is the law of belief. A belief is a thought in your mind. Do not believe in things to harm or hurt you. Believe in the power of your subconscious to heal, inspire, strengthen, and prosper you. According to your belief is it done unto you.

10. Change your thoughts, and you change your destiny.

"Realize the marvelous powers of Your Subconscious Mind", and make the best use to your advantage.

You inert abilities can bring more confidence, more power, maybe strive wealth, better health, attain happiness, and get joy by learning to contact and release the hidden power of your subconscious mind.

"The possibilities of creative effort connected with the subconscious

mind are stupendous and imponderable.

They inspire one with awe."

—*Napoleon Hill*

Chapter 3

Use Amazing Powers of Creativity & Lateral Thinking

Creativity and Lateral thinking are two different types of activities which our Mind carries out. Both are amazing abilities that one can have. **Both are special skills which you can develop and gain huge advantage.**

In Creativity the common element is production of something new. Example, a Scientists are said to be creative if they make a new discovery, new invention, new products are all are creative.

Whereas in Lateral Thinking, the brain is engaged in evolving patterns but sticking to the main idea. Re-engineering, Re-design, Remapping etc

Creativity enables formation of New Ideas, "it defies Logic in Creating New thing/What", whereas in Lateral thinking the Focus is "Possible/ may be .. Why/ Where" the ideas do not defy each other but co-exist.

Edward De Bono, pioneer of Brain Training, has been a tireless advocate for the value of creative thinking, and he deserves credit for helping to push creativity to the forefront , but a key aim of lateral thinking is to deliberately and systematically create those unrelated concepts and then force them together.

Lateral Thinking is essential. Instead of linear or vertical thinking, which relies solely on logic, Lateral Thinking is a deliberate, systematic process of using your ability to think in a different way. By Mind Power, we usually mean the overall capacity of the mind. It can be expressed in many ways, some of which are listed below:

- Cognitive Abilities
- Intelligence
- Paranormal Mind Powers
- Creativity
- Talents
- Way of Thinking
- Consciousness
- Intuition

The Definition of Creativity

It is the ability to transcend traditional ideas, rules, patterns, relationships, or the like, and to create meaningful new ideas, forms, methods, interpretations, etc.; originality, progressiveness, or imagination.

Creativity involves breaking out of established patterns in order to look at things in a different way - Edward de Bono.

Creativity is the mental characteristic that allows a person to think outside the box, which results in innovative or different approaches to a particular task. It is the ability to produce original and unusual ideas, or to make something new or imaginative.

There is no doubt that creativity is the most important human resource of all. Without creativity, there would be no progress, and we would be forever repeating the same patterns- Edward de Bono.

The Logic of Creativity

Albert Einstein said "Creativity is intelligence having fun"

In 1969 De Bono wrote a book called "The Mechanism of Mind". In that book he described how the nerve networks in the brain allow incoming information to organize itself into sequence or patterns.

What it amounts to is that there are two broad types of information systems: the passive system and the active system. Almost all our usual systems (including computers) are of the passive type. Information is recorded on a surface and lies there passively until it is used by some brain or central processor. The surface and the information or data are entirely passive. In the active system, on the other hand, the information and the surface are both active.

Our self-organizing systems set up patterns. Such patterns are usually asymmetric. This means that we normally go along the main track without even noticing the side track. But, if-somehow-we get across to the side track, the route becomes obvious in hindsight. This is the basis of both humor and creativity.

The Process of Developing Creativity: Your innovative Prowess

De Bono's Book *Art of transcending Creativity*, follows a systematic learning and described the Creativity process as follows:

Evolve

- Shattering the common myths around creative thinking
- Understanding the logic of creativity
- Think outside the box
- Unfold new ideas

Focus

- Shifting from the single focus on problems
- Learning the importance of redefining the focus
- Developing your own creative list/hit list of ideas

Challenge

- Challenging traditional ways constructively
- Learning to break free of our thinking patterns

Alternatives

- Learning the 'how to' and value of extracting concepts

- Using concepts to breed new ideas

Random Entry

- Using random thoughts/input to create new connections
- New connections generate new activities

Provocation

- Going beyond deferring judgment to active movement
- Turning provocative ideas into practical solutions

Our minds have been trained to find typical and predictable solutions to problems. Often this leads to 'thinking inside the box' and to entrapment in old paradigms.

In challenging old paradigms and using Dr. Edward de Bono's Lateral Thinking methods, a DuPont employee eliminated nine steps in their Kevlar manufacturing process and saved the company $30 million. More clearly you see that learning to think deliberately 'outside the box' pays off.

From strategic planning to solutions for everyday issues, thousands of individuals worldwide have used this proven method to create and have innovative breakthroughs.

Create Creativity Hit-list to "Generate Outcomes"

- Shatter the myths around creative thinking - you can do it, and do it better.
- Bring your creative thinking and the thinking of others into a sharp focus.
- Develop your own creative list of new ideas called 'hit list'.
- Find and build on the concept behind one idea to create even more ideas.
- Spark new ideas by random and uncommon inputs.
- Go beyond deferring judgement to active movement.
- Use provocative questions to challenge current thinking.
- Turn provocative ideas into new and practical solutions.

- Challenge your organization's current thinking constructively and productively.
- Turn harvested ideas into usable, practical forms.
- Maximize the ideas you capture from creative thinking.
- Be creative on demand.

In evolving Creativity, we need to overcome several misconceptions:

- "You have to be an artist to be creative."
- "Ideas have always happened."
- "Creativity is a talent that some people have and others do not."
- "Creativity comes from rebels."
- "Being liberated is enough."
- "Tools and techniques are confining."

Improving Creativity: 5 Step Process

Bryan Collins, Author of Power of Creativity mentions that improving creativity often involves knowing how your brain works best and utilizing techniques in your thinking that will allow access to your rich, most creative mind space.

While some aspects of creative thinking are different for everyone, many depend on how the brain itself works.

Step 1. Idea Generation and Research

- Brainstorm
- Do research
- Gain resources
- Enrich with Ideas
- Unorthodox ideas ok

To generate them, you need to perform research, collect information, look for relationships between resources, and analyze.

You can assimilate or borrow ideas from resources with similar problems and generate fresh ideas based on them.

"Creativity is just connecting things. Creative people see things and do it. Brainstorming process is obvious to them with natural flow of Ideas"
- Steve Jobs

Step 2. Combine the Thoughts

Look for relationships between the materials you have collected.

Now it's time to work with the material you've collected. To help an idea form, do the following:

- Narrow down the best resources from what you've found.
- Specify connections between them.
- Think of new connections.
- Brainstorm.

Step 3. Reveal the Sub consciousness

- Here comes the most creative part of your idea generation process: while brainstorming, forget about the subject and let your sub consciousness work.
- Techniques to try:
- Brainstorming in a group with your peers;
- Mind mapping: use graphics to draw connections between ideas and pieces of information you have;
- Free writing: just pick up a pen and write the streamline of thoughts that helps to express your subconscious ideas.
- So, in this step we step away from the subject and let your subconscious genius work.

Step 4. Reach Your "A-Ha Moment"

"Just think about it, deeply, and then forget it. An idea will…jump up in your face." – Don Draper
- That's what James Webb Young calls an "a-ha moment" when your brilliant idea appears out of nowhere. Once you forget about the core subject and change perspective, you may be surprised.
- How to change perspective?

- Imagine yourself an opossum. Or pencil. Or Madonna. What would they say on the topic?
- Run in the park, take a shower, take a seat in front of some picture and stare at it for a while, whatever.
- Enjoy the process, don't be in a hurry. (Now you understand why you should plan your academic writing well in advance, don't you?)

So, your fourth step to idea generation: don't miss an "a-ha moment"!

Here we tickle your brain for great job done when appreciation is made and thereby raises the Power of Sub consciousness to great latency.

Step 5. Evaluate

Once the idea strikes you, work on its evaluation and improvement, make sure that:

- It is raw concepts fit your core subject;
- Your presentation of the idea won't look like a plagiarism;
- it fits your academic performance. (But no one forbids improving it, after all).

So, your final step to idea generation: evaluate and improve it.

Continuous Improvement

Continuous Improvement for creative ideas happens when subconscious activity of the brain is appreciated. Creativity adrenaline flows into the brain and allows progressive repetitive activities to generate more creative Ideas. Continuous Improvement takes place within the brain factory and produces more creative- "A-ha" moments.

Creativity is Ubiquitous

The "Creativity at work" blog says Creativity is the act of turning new and imaginative ideas into reality. Wikipedia on Creativity says that "Creativity is a phenomenon whereby something new or somehow valuable is formed". The created item is usually intangible.

Definition of Lateral Thinking

Lateral thinking... is the process of using information to bring about creativity and insight restructuring. Lateral thinking can be learned, practiced and used. It is possible to acquire skill in it just as it is possible to acquire skill in mathematics. Edward de Bono.

De Bono has described a number of ways of defining Lateral Thinking.

- *"You cannot dig a hole in a different place by digging the same hole deeper."*
- *"Lateral Thinking is for changing concepts and perceptions instead of trying harder with the same concepts and perceptions."*
- *"In self-organizing information systems, asymmetric patterns are formed. Lateral Thinking is a method for cutting across from one pattern to another."*

Prudence of Lateral Thinking

The first difficulty is to get time and space for lateral thinking. There are those who think that lateral thinking is only for special brainstorming sessions. There are those who believe that lateral is not for them but for artists, designers and inventors. This is a dangerous and limiting attitude. Anyone can practice Lateral thinking and can get better.

Just as the ability to use the reverse shift is part of every driver's driving ability, the ability to use lateral thinking should be part of every thinker's thinking skill. Lateral thinking is definitely not limited to special people or special occasions.

The logic of perception demands the ability to think laterally, so anyone who has to do any thinking must develop this ability.

6 Hats Technique

In order to make creative thinking part of ordinary thinking, De Bono developed the Six Thinking Hats system. There are six metaphorical hats in colors of White, Black, Red, Blue, Green and Yellow. The thinker can put one on or take one off to indicate the type of thinking that is being used. This putting on and taking off is essential. The hats must never be used to categorize individuals, even though their behavior may seem to invite this.

An individual can express his or her thoughts under the protection of one or the other hats. For example, someone might say: "Wearing my red hat, I think that idea is exciting. I cannot tell you exactly why, but I have that feeling about it." Someone else might preface a negative input by declaring that some black hat thinking is needed. An individual can ask a whole group to adopt a hat for a limited period of time. For example, at a meeting someone might suggest: "What we need here is three minutes of green hat thinking."

I am not suggesting that in every moment in thinking there is a need to wear one of the hats. The hats provide an opportunity to switch thinking. In the course of an ordinary discussion someone might say: "Let's have three minutes of black hat thinking here." At the end of the three minutes, the discussion would resume as before.

Sometimes it is possible to put together a formal sequence of hats in order to think productively about some matter. The actual order of the sequence will vary with the situation. For example, with a new matter, the sequence might be: white (to get information); green (for ideas and proposals); yellow followed by black on each alternative (to evaluate the alternatives); red (to assess feelings at this point); followed by blue (to decide what thinking to do next). On the other hand, in discussing a well known proposal, the sequence might run: red, yellow, black, green (to overcome the negative points), white, and then blue.

Lateral Thinking People are never short of Ideas. Over the years, many people who are highly creative in their own fields have said they get the best ideas when they use the Lateral Thinking tools systematically. Such people are never short of ideas, but they surprise themselves with a new idea only when they use the tools deliberately.

We can either drown in this information or turn it into a lifesaver by extracting its practical knowledge. Neuroplasticity is the ability of the brain to continuously create new neural pathways.

The same happens physically in the brain whether we perform the action, or simply visualize it-Your brain cannot tell the difference between an action you performed and an action you visualized.

Albert Einstein is credited with saying that "imagination is more important than knowledge".

In a Harvard University study, two groups of volunteers were presented with a piece of unfamiliar piano music. One group received the music and a keyboard, and was told to practice. The other group was instructed to just read the music and imagine playing it. When their brain activity was examined, both groups showed expansion in their motor cortex, even though the second group had never touched a keyboard!

Parker J. Palmer, founder of the Center for Courage and Renewal once said, "Science requires an engagement with the world, a live encounter between the knower and the known." *In other words, knowing is not enough. We do ourselves and others a great disservice when we don't decide to act on the gift of knowledge.* It's the difference between hoarding information and developing wisdom."

Let's take a look at a well-known pharmaceutical company which used Lateral Thinking Tools to Power Idea Generation. Jeffrey Wall, the Managing Partner with The Value Enablement Group, was an Enterprise Architect at the time. His company was using the Kaizen method for process improvement and Jeffrey, a certified Lateral Thinking trainer and facilitator, realized that the Lateral Thinking method could address several needs. Employees were taught the Kaizen method along with selected Lateral Thinking tools; which included initial core dump of ideas, followed by random selection of lateral ideas, then finishing up with Challenges to solve. This enabled Process to reach more diverse thinking for transformational ideas and better Production systems.

The results were significant in that the team generated some 200 ideas covering 30 concepts using a total time commitment of less than 3 hours. The senior members of the team then leveraged their domain knowledge to identify which opportunities were best suited to achieve their objectives.

The combined Kaizen & Lateral Thinking exercise yielded a 50% projected reduction in cycle time. Many of the short-term ideas were implemented within a week (as there were no resource requirements). The team was able to demonstrate improvement in a number of areas throughout the product development lifecycle.

Lateral Thinking produces a wide range of ideas, some of which may lead to disruptive innovation.

These ideas must be captured and funneled into a process for further assessment, planning, and potential implementation.

- A plan for assessing ideas and aligning ideas to address desired customer outcomes.
- A process for prioritizing ideas to ensure there is an appropriate blend of balancing short-term needs (outcomes) while lining up investments (bigger ideas) to address long-term needs (outcomes)
- A capability for building value-driven business cases will ensure that the bigger ideas are addressing highly unmet needs of customers. This will also help align the necessary support to engage in strategic experiments to move these ideas forward while managing risk and investments with care.
- And new approaches for encouraging an open mindset where these experiments can move forward so that the bigger ideas get transitioned into the execution pipeline.

Ultimately Jeffrey was so encouraged by the results of this experience and others that he had while involved with the Innovation Center that he saw the possibilities of applying these combined techniques in other organizations. To pursue this goal, Jeffrey has established his own consulting firm, The Value Enablement Group. This Group has helped organizations drive innovation, agility, simplicity, and Operational excellence by encouraging Lateral thing and the Powers of Creativity.

Synergy of Creativity and Lateral Thinking is a game changer

This synergy can be very productive and a game changer when you combine the two; Creativity and Lateral Thinking are both superlatives attributes which can make you extremely successful and Lead from the front.

- Creativity examples = Thinking outside the box, Unusual, New, Original, Innovation, Imaginative, Rational/Irrational, Unrelated, in other words try something different even if you know it won't work in other words "Beyond Common Wisdom"
- Lateral Thinking examples =Reengineering, creative revision, Restructuring, Process improvement, Functional improvements, Refine tasks, Technical Enhancements, Operational Efficiencies , in other words "Critical Insight /For Common Good"

Creativity and Lateral Thinking together, "creates a synergy of Excellence" that can lead to new ideas.

This can lead to Individual linear behavior, Developing new ideas, Solves common problems, Product Ideas/Development, Process Improvement, Transformation of Application, Time Optimization, Technically and Functionally strengthens into brand new concepts, and new awakening etc.

Pablo Picasso changed art forever by smashing the "rules" of perspective, color, and proportion. His Cubism took hold in Paris faster than Van Gogh's impressionism—and any other new form, for that matter.

Apple turned the tech world on its head by radically simplifying music with their iTunes Store, the menu options in the bar will sometimes change location after you click them.

This synergy of Creative Ideas and Lateral Thinking resolves complex issues, generates excellences and creative solutions, with your Center of Excellence. It is a tremendous boon for your success and eminence.

"Excellence is a

Common thing in an uncommon way"

—Booker T. Washington

Chapter 4

Attain Happiness: The 6 Keys

> What you think, you become.
>
> What you feel, you attract.
>
> What you imagine, you create.
>
> -BUDDHA

"As a result of contentment, you gain happiness." -Yoga Sutra 42, Chapter II
"How to Know God" the Yoga Aphorisms of Patanjali.

Why should you be happy?

Happiness is extremely important to us, both as individuals and as a world, primarily because happiness is really all there is. As human beings, although we possess cognitive abilities and are highly "thought" oriented, *the Quality of our lives is ultimately ENTIRELY determined by our emotions.*

The fundamental reason why happiness is so important is that, it's extremely vital to our own goals in life and can help us achieve many other cherished personal ambitions and goals. Also, by being happy; we have the potential to change many other lives just by being ourselves.

For example, which life would you rather have; that of a very rich, attractive, successful, healthy, powerful person who despite all of those blessings is very unhappy or that of a very poor, unattractive, unsuccessful, unhealthy and powerless person who is nevertheless fortunate enough to be very happy?

Psychologically, being happy makes us happy, I mean it makes us feel good. It releases positive hormones in the body. It is life giving. The whole mechanics in the body makes it a positive experience and our mind wants to experience it again and again.

We somewhere believe that happiness is difficult to achieve. And we always run for things that are difficult to achieve, so it becomes a constant "pursuit of happiness". We set personal goals and believe that achieving these goals would make us happy. So, constant pursuit of happiness gives a meaning to our life.

Spiritually, we want to be happy because that is the inherent nature of the soul that we have. Bliss means a state beyond happiness. It is a state of purity, of inner peace which is always there. We actually aim for all these aspects. Somewhere they relate to the Maslow's hierarchy as well.

- Physical need means food
- Energy is life, air, the vital force that keeps us alive
- Mental refers to our mind, our emotions
- Wisdom is the knowledge we strive for
- Bliss is the happiness (per Vedanta).

"We become happier when we live in the depth of the present moment-with no regrets of the past and no worry of the future"- The great father of yoga, Patanjali, says this is what is meant by contentment.

Patanjali also mentions that "happiness" comes from the satisfaction of a desire. This may become vivid but short lived as the satisfaction of one desire soon leads to the rise of another and so the moment of happiness may end in anxiety.

The line that comforts me the most is: God is always with us.

That love may be released at any moment by letting go of fear and desires that may shield this love.

Just how happy do we need to be? It turns out that among very happy people, those who are a tad less joyful than the happiest of happy actually have higher incomes, academic achievement, job satisfaction, and political participation than the happiest people.

Common belief suggests that happiness is a type of "Nirvana" which we should never lose hope of attaining. It's something like a state of fulfillment and constant bliss.

"Happiness is realizing that nothing is too important." Antonio Gala

On achieving Happiness: Create Positive Center of Excellence

Positive Center of Excellence utilizes evidence-based practices; create quality internal systems to promote high staff satisfaction, high client satisfaction and positive outcomes for those they service.

A study conducted by Harvard University by the professor Tal Ben-Shahar, expert in positive psychology, shows that joy can be learned! The means to acquire this knowledge is the same as to attain any other skill: technique and practice matters.

Positive Psychology brings together studies of happiness in both science and nature, to provide knowledge of how to find true happiness and contentment. Positive Psychology helps you to change your life and leads you to a **positive Center of Excellence**. It helps to shape your Beliefs and Adds Value to your life.

Happiness is based on State of Mind, and can be classified into 6 Keys.

The 6 Keys to "Attain Happiness"

1. Learn to celebrate your failures

I do believe that if you haven't learnt about failures, you cannot appreciate success. Nana Mouskouri

People who are more capable of positively valuing their failures tend to be happier people. It's very harmful to believe that you are infallible or to suppose that you don't have the right to make mistakes.

But, besides this, it's about an idealist and tyrannical view we hold against ourselves.

45

Aren't mistakes our daily bread? Hasn't science itself, which is a mode of thoroughness and perfection, been riddled with mistakes through the course of history?

"Do not judge me by my success, judge me by how many times I fell down and got back up again." Nelson Mandela.

Thinking that we can't or shouldn't make mistakes, is an unfounded idea that only produces anxiety and depression.

2. Be thankful for what you have

"Be happy for this moment. This moment is your life" Omar Khayyam

You may believe that your health, your family or your work are realities that will be there forever, and that's why you don't grant them an important value in your life. You take for granted that they're a part of your assets and forget that in one breath you can lose any of them.

It's very true that daily we forget to be grateful for all of those daily miracles that seem "normal" to us. Unfortunately, we notice their immense value only when they're no longer there and we realize just how important they were.

3. Joy release Endorphins: Be Joyful

"Joy is prayer; joy is strength: joy is love; joy is a net of love by which you can catch soul". Mother Teresa

Endorphins are the hormones of happiness. They can be found within our brains and are always at our disposal. We just don't know how to use them. A daily 30 minute walk can help release sufficient doses of endorphins Moreover, simply imagining hugging a person you love the most can cause your brain to release serotonin, dopamine, and endorphin, triggering feelings of happiness and joy.

It's simple: if you get into the habit of doing activities that promote the release of endorphins, you'll surely feel more joy.

4. Simplify your life

Today I choose life. Every morning when I wake up I can choose joy, happiness, negativity, pain... To feel the freedom that comes from being able to continue to make mistakes and choices - today I choose to feel life, not to deny my humanity but embrace it. Kevyn Aucoin

It's true that you only live once. But this doesn't mean that you should try to live everything at once. One of today's most common illnesses wants to do too many things at once and hopefully all of them swiftly. Your physical and mental health can't take such a desperate way of life for very long.

Learn to get organized. Give each activity its own time and value. Eliminate all of the tasks that rob you of precious life moments.

Make your life simple to manage Time well. Instead, taking time away from yourself and the people you love most can have a very high price.

5. Practice Meditation

"Meditation brings wisdom; lack of meditation leaves ignorance. Know well what leads you forward and what holds you back, and choose the path that leads to wisdom." –Buddha

There's no need for you to become a Tibetan monk. It's enough to take a few minutes each day to find balance, through the practice of simple meditation.

Meditation has proven to be a great way of achieving inner peace. It also helps achieve better cognitive and creative functions and a high power of will.

6. Cultivate Resilience

"The best people possess a feeling for beauty, the courage to take risks, the discipline to tell the truth, the capacity for sacrifice. Ironically, their virtues make them vulnerable; they are often wounded, sometimes destroyed." Ernest Hemingway.

Yes, resilience can be cultivated. It's not an innate ability, but rather one you can develop. It's defined as the ability of facing adverse situations and leaving them as stronger people.

In order to be resilient you have to put in real effort. You need to focus on finding the flower in the mud: the lesson in the middle of difficulty. It's the path to wisdom and happiness.

To boost resiliency, Dr. Emma Seppala of Stanford mentions "focus on your breathing. Breathe is something we can control and yet most of the time it happens unconsciously without our effort"

No surprise - happiness is not just derived from worldly possessions, but it is more absolute which comes from peace within, from satisfaction of your mind and spiritual providence, as 'Ah-ha" moment of your life.

These "6 Keys to Happiness" are a series of useful practices, to help promote a sense of joy and contentment in your everyday life.

"It is better to conquer yourself,

than to win a thousand battles.

Then the victory is yours.

It cannot be taken from you"

—Lord Buddha

Chapter 5

Treasure "12 Laws of Karma" that will change your life

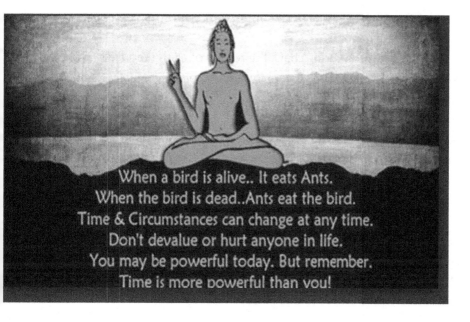

When a bird is alive.. It eats Ants.
When the bird is dead..Ants eat the bird.
Time & Circumstances can change at any time.
Don't devalue or hurt anyone in life.
You may be powerful today. But remember.
Time is more powerful than you!

What is Karma? Karma is the Sanskrit word for action. It is equivalent to Newton's law of 'every action must have a reaction'.

When we think, speak or act we initiate a force that will react accordingly. This returning force maybe modified, changed or suspended, but most people will not be able eradicate it.

"You have to trust in something - your gut, destiny, life, karma, whatever. This approach has never let me down, and it has made all the difference in my life"- Steve Jobs

A person may not escape the consequences of his actions, but he will suffer only if he himself has made the conditions ripe for his suffering. Ignorance of the law is no excuse whether the laws are man-made or universal.

"The Law of Karma in the moral sphere teaches that similar actions will lead to similar results", per facets of Buddhism 'The Law of Karma and Mindfulness'.

To stop being afraid and to start being empowered in the worlds of karma and reincarnation, here is what you need to know about karmic laws.

Role of Karma in Center of Excellence of your life

Karma is the law that brings back the results of all the thoughts, words, and actions to our lives. It plays a very important role perpetually to inspire the highest excellence in our life.

When you understand the concept of karma, you will see that whatsoever is happening to you is really of your own doing. Nothing happens to you from outside of you. You create whatever happens to you.

Creating Center of Excellence enables as to how Good health, Good values and beliefs can enable a person to live a life full of meaning, transform others and attain happiness That is attaining purity of mind through selfless service and selflessness. For excellence in life's work we have to control our minds for the requisite concentration to be achieved.

The twelve laws of karma encompass cause and effect - an unbreakable law of the cosmos, some of which can guide us to achieve the life that we desire:

12 Laws of Karma

1. THE GREAT LAW

– "As you sow, so shall you reap". This is also known as the "Law of Cause and Effect".
– Whatever we put out in the Universe is what comes back to us

– If what we want is Happiness, Peace, Love, Friendship, then we should BE Happy, Peaceful, Loving and a True Friend

"Before the reward there must be labor. You plant before you harvest. You sow in tears before you reap joy". Ralph Ransom

2. THE LAW OF CREATION

– Life doesn't just HAPPEN, it requires our participation.
– We are one with the Universe, both inside and out.
– Whatever surrounds us gives us clues to our inner state.
– BE yourself, and surround yourself with what you want to have present in your Life. Problems or successes, they all are the results of our own actions. Karma.

"The philosophy of action is that no one else is the giver of peace or happiness. One's own karma, one's own actions are responsible to come to bring either happiness or success or whatever" Maharishi Mahesh Yogi

3. THE LAW OF HUMILITY

– What you refuse to accept; will continue for you.
– If what we see is an enemy, or someone with a character trait that we find to be negative, then we ourselves are not focused on a higher level of existence.

"I guess one of the ways that karma works is that it finds out what you are most afraid of and then makes that happen eventually". Cheech Marin

4. THE LAW OF GROWTH

– "Wherever you go, there you are".
– For us to GROW in Spirit, it is we who must change – and not the people, places or things around us.
– The only given we have in our lives is OURSELVES and that is the only factor we have control over.
– When we change who and what we are within our heart our life follows suit and changes too.

"My mother believed in curses, karma, good luck, bad luck, Feng shui. Her amorphous set of beliefs showed me you can pick and choose the qualities of your philosophy, based on what works for you". Amy Tan

5. THE LAW OF RESPONSIBILITY

– Whenever there is something wrong in my life, there is something wrong in me.
– We mirror what surrounds us – and what surrounds us mirrors us; this is a Universal Truth.
– We must take responsibility what is in our life.

"Karma brings us ever back to rebirth, binds us to the wheel of births and deaths. Good Karma drags us back as relentlessly as bad, and the chain which is wrought out of our virtues holds as firmly and as closely as that forged from our vices". Annie Besant

6. THE LAW OF CONNECTION

– Even if something we do seems inconsequential, it is very important that it gets done as everything in the Universe is connected.
– Each step leads to the next step, and so forth and so on.
– Someone must do the initial work to get a job done.
– Neither the first step nor the last are of greater significance, as they were both needed to accomplish the task.
– Past-Present-Future they are all connected

"When someone has a strong intuitive connection, Buddhism suggests that it's because of karma, some past connection" Richard Gere

7. THE LAW OF FOCUS

– You cannot think of two things at the same time.
– When our focus is on Spiritual Values, it is impossible for us to have lower thoughts such as greed or anger.

"Things don't just happen in this world of arising and passing away. We don't live in some kind of crazy, accidental universe. Things happen for a reason. They happen according to certain laws, laws of nature" Sharon Salzberg

8. THE LAW OF GIVING AND HOSPITALITY

– If you believe something to be true, then sometime in your life you will be called upon to demonstrate that particular truth.
– Here is where we put what we CLAIM that we have learned, into actual PRACTICE.

"I definitely consider myself a Christian. There are things that I believe in, there are things I have a self-belief on. I know I got a great relationship with God and the universe. I just believe in being a righteous person and karma. Doing unto others as you would have done unto you. I really want to help teach that".   *Big Sean*

9. THE LAW OF HERE AND NOW

– Looking backward to examine what was, prevents us from being totally in the HERE AND NOW.
– Old thoughts, old patterns of behavior, old dreams...
– Prevent us from having new ones.

"There's a natural law of karma that vindictive people, who go out of their way to hurt others, will end up broke and alone" *Sylvester Stallone*

10. THE LAW OF CHANGE

– History repeats itself until we learn the lessons that we need to change our path.

"I don't know what religious people do. I kind of wished I'd been a Christian with the blind faith that God is doing the right thing. As a Buddhist, you feel like you have more control over the situation, and that you can change your karma". *Marcia Wallace*

11. THE LAW OF PATIENCE AND REWARD

– All Rewards require initial toil.
– Rewards of lasting value require patient and persistent toil.

– True joy follows doing what we're supposed to be doing, and waiting for the reward to come in on its own time.

"I've really been extremely lucky. Some people work just as hard, are just as intelligent, and they don't get their breaks. I've just gotten the breaks. Maybe it's good karma" Jorge M. Perez

12. THE LAW OF SIGNIFICANCE AND INSPIRATION

– You get back from something whatever YOU have put into it.
– The true value of something is a direct result of the energy and intent that is put into it.
– Every personal contribution is also a contribution to the Whole.
– Lack luster contributions have no impact on the Whole, nor do they work to diminish it.
– Loving contributions bring life to, and inspire, the Whole.

"Someone is sitting in the shade today because someone planted a tree a long time ago "Warren Buffet.

These "12 laws of karma" have stood the test of time and proved true as they have ever been.

Follow these simple laws and enjoy your evolved life.

"Problems or successes,
they all are the results of our own actions Karma.
The philosophy of action is that,
No one else is the giver of peace or happiness.
One's own karma,
one's own actions are responsible
To come to bring either
happiness or success"

—Maharishi Mahesh Yogi

PART TWO

TAKE THE PATH:

MAKE

OUTSTANDING

THINGS HAPPEN

Chapter 6

Create the Unexpected by Making

Difficult things Possible

Life is a Journey of Unexpected and we are constantly Navigating through the struggles, travails of life and circumstances. *It is Our attitude that matters*.

A Positive Attitude enables a person to Win Battle and a Negative attitude Begets Depressions.

"Your success and happiness lies in you. Resolve to keep happy, and your joy and you shall form an invincible host against difficulties" Helen Keller.

We all come across various difficulties in our lives. However, not all of us handle them as effectively as we should. As strategies for getting through life's problems are rarely formally learned in school, so we are constrained to use trial and error, sometimes leading to sub-optimal results.

Overcoming difficulties by Creative Effort, with A Will to Succeed

"Creativity is inventing, experimenting, growing, taking risks, breaking rules, making mistakes, and having fun." Mary Lou Cook

I will like to share my story of as to how I was able to overcome some very difficult challenges in India, one of the world's largest democracies. Times were plagued with Bureaucracy and Red-tapism, and how I fought with the laws of the land, worked through with tenacity and sense of purpose, and creative efforts, **launched the Export of Steel In India for the First time in 1991.**

This created a History of sorts, where Private Sector created quality Product, Raising the bar of Excellence and Exporting it, thereby entering into the World stage, into the "Big Arena of Global competition and Excellence".

Saga: How I "Created the Unexpected in very difficult conditions":

The Prologue of Indian Steel industry before 1991

India produced 14.34 million tons in 1991-92 where Steel Production had 100% domestic consumption. The quality was not really a matter of consideration as it was a Sellers' Market. There were local buyers of all grades of Steel Products. Government had major control over the majority of Steel plants and, raw material production, but was riddled with bureaucratic rigmaroles.

Leading the crusade at all levels for "Creation of Export Policy".

Till 1991, the export of Steel was banned. I fought the battle at all levels right from basic Concept selling to Export of Product, validating with various tenacious and bureaucratic authorities, pursued New Policy creation for Exports and ensured our Quality standards were met in the International Market.

I recall I had some serious initial challenges to overcome. To begin with:

- There was no Export Policy in the Country to Export Steel.
- Steel Ministry was bureaucratic and Public Sector centric.
- CCIE (Chief Controller for Imports and Exports) approval for Exports was not there.
- Import of Raw Material was Red-taped-restricted/License based.
- There were no DGTD Technical Input/Output Norms for Raw material vs Export Product.
- There were no ISO 9000 norms available for Inspection for Exports in the country.

It was a grand vision of Mr. Sajjan Jindal (Chairman and Managing Director of Jindal Group), who happened to meet me in a flight from Delhi to Bombay and during the discussions he came up an idea to Export the Steel. He wanted me to Lead and drives it from end to end, turn all stones and Make it Happen. I had some personal challenges, I would have to switch jobs, as I was doing well with my earlier company for 9+ years, and they refused to accept my resignation. However Mr. Jindal ensured that the transition took place. That story is also amazing, a triumph over odds.

All credit to him for his great vision and belief in me. Despite the fact he was fully aware, that the Government of India has no Policy for Exports, we had to face Bureaucratic rigmaroles and we did not even have proper raw materials to manufacture to begin with. We had to not only adhere to tough International ISO 9000 standards but also face the stiff International Price competition. He believed that if we have an Attitude to Success, we can make it Happen.

When I joined Jindal Group in May 1991, we did not even have an Export Dept. I set it up from scratch and started with selection of few individuals who could made a good team, where we all were committed to doing whatever it would takes to get this job done and take this onerous task forward.

We all believed: "Make difficult things possible, Take one Step at a time".

The odds ware heavy and this was no mean task. We had to start from scratch. Setting up exports initiative with such a massive bureaucratic framework was not easy. This was the first time ever where there was an effort by any private sector group in the country.

Externally we fought at all levels right from the Steel Ministry, CCIE, DGTD and Licensing authorities to convince them of the Exports concept and then creation of Policy by the Government of India for Exports. We conceived technical data for Import of Raw Material, created Technical Norms for Product Specification, and created Input and Out norms for DGTD etc. huge steps made and a lot of difficulties faced at all levels.

My whole team knew the odds were up, but were all committed to success. When we did some initial production quality run based on domestic raw material there was huge wastage. The international quality standards were not close. So we decided to import suitable raw material to manufacture desired Hot Rolled Plates-the Export product. We collected International specifications for Exports. We approached several International exporters which included Japanese and Korean groups for samples, who were world leaders. We imported several samples and took to our quality lab. Thereon we created a new attitude by changing the Quality Dept. from Quality Acceptance to Quality Assurance and raised the bar of quality. Positive Attitude matters.

On the parallel front, we fought the battle with the Steel Ministry, the Government of India, the DGTD and the CCIE offices of the Government of India.

After herculean convincing and parlaying, we were able to get the permission to export which was granted, that was the first time in history of the country. That was huge victory for our efforts.

Then we worked with our Manufacturing Division to produce suitable Export product, which was possible after a lot of QA measures to do things right. Then we worked with SGS, an International Inspection company to set up ISO 9000 norms (again for the first time in the country). Finally we produced the product with the desired export quality, met the International ISO 9000 standards and exported the product with a great sense of accomplishment.

Overall sustained efforts created "History of Sorts within 6 months":

- May 1991: Joined Jindal Group
- Set up Export Division in Jindal Group
- Steel Ministry agreed to allow private sector to export after great persuasions
- Govt of India amended Export Import Policy to accommodate this Export of Product
- DGTD Created norms for input/output for Steel Exports
- Govt of India agreed to give permission to Jindal Group to Export
- CCIE Issued a License to Jindal Group to Import suitable Raw material
- We created ISO 9000 norms with help of SGS to meet Export standards
- Nov 1991 Jindal Group Exported Steel (Hot Rolled Plates) for the first time in the history of India

That was a giant step towards Liberalization and Globalization in India. This Success turned the pages of History and future of Steel Industry in India.

Indian iron and steel sector became the first core sector to be deregulated in 1991. The de-reservation of capacity was followed by de-control of price and distribution. The lowering of tariff rates and lifting of quantitative restrictions were steps towards further liberalization. The post liberalization era witnessed the emergence of private sector. Financial institutions cleared 19 projects of 13 million tons with an investment of US $1 billion.

Global integration and Research and Development became the key to increase productivity and ensure quality, cost effectiveness, safety and an environmentally friendly atmosphere in the steel plants.

Today the Steel Ministry has been pursuing the industry to make more investments in this area. As per the decision of the Government, R&D activities were supplemented by the Steel Ministry by providing financial assistance from the Steel Development Fund (SDF). The Ministry has set up an Institute for Steel Development & Growth (INSDAG) and a National Campaign Committee under the Joint Plant Committee for the promotion of steel. The Steel Ministry later also decided to set up an apex organization "The National Steel Institute" for the promotion of Research, Training and Consultancy in the Steel Sector. This was a massive thrust towards the huge presence of the Industry in the face of globalization.

The nineties witnessed the largest expansion of capacity and output of steel sector. The production of steel increased from 14.34 million tons in 1991-92 to over 95.8 million tons in 2015-2016.Today India ranks 3rd largest in a global steel production in the world after China and the USA. India is now the 14th largest Exporter in the world exporting about 10 million tons of steel in 2015-2016 worth US $ 6.3 billion and Exports accounting for 10.5% of total Production.

Today India exports steel to more than 200 countries, due to this liberalization and deregulation that started in 1991-92.

The provisions of this policy allowed private sector participation to set up plants with large capacities. The Iron and steel industry was included in the high priority list for foreign investments thus, encouraging global participation. This led to greater access not only to information on global operations /techniques in manufacturing but also opening up new channels of procuring inputs as well as newer markets for selling the end products and territories worldwide (Growth of Indian steel industry and challenges by H.K.Jain, ED SAIL CET and Jagdish Arora, AGM (T), Centre For Engineering and Technology SAIL, Ranchi, India).

One Giant step made in 1991, made huge strides into the future.

It was sheer difficulty that was overcome by hard work, a creative effort to create something unexpected and providing the initial thrust for "Getting Things Done".

This was possible by an Attitude to create the Unexpected by making difficult things Possible, an extraordinary effort in the right direction.

We all have obstacles to overcome, some are major and some minor. We have to govern our attitude to create something new, something different. The path is not easy, it is difficult.

So if we have the Will and Positive Attitude, we can make impossible things look possible.

Important Learnings from this difficult task; Positive Attitude Matters

There is very important attitude dimension that enables us to handle and solve life's difficult problems:

- *The first is that everything happens for your own good; nothing negative happens. All events contain an advantage for you if you look for it.*
- *See the positive in all and everything. We need to be able to apply this attitude in every event, problem and challenge that we encounter, regardless of whether we like them or not.*
- *We need to have the ability to catch the opportunity.*
- *Like and dislike are always there, we should stay positive.*
- *If we can find the message, catch the hidden advantage, the positive aspect of the experience, and hold that mentality, then,*
- *Even though we may not understand fully, we have made a great start towards handling the different challenges we have to face.*

5 Step Process to Solve Difficult Problems

Problem solving is a critical skill for success for all at all fronts

People tend to do three things when faced with a problem: they become afraid or uncomfortable and wish it would go away; they feel that they have to come up with an answer and it has to be the right answer; and they look for someone to blame. Being faced with a problem becomes a problem. And that's a problem because, in fact, there are always going to be problems!

The most common mistake in problem solving is trying to find a solution right away. That's a mistake because it tries to put the solution at the beginning of the process, when what we need is a solution at the end of process.

Problem solving characterizes the steps that can be followed by any discipline when approaching and rationally solving a problem.

5 Step Process to solve your difficult Problems

1. Define the Problem

Identify the Cause or Issue.

Input: something is wrong or something could be improved.

What are you trying to solve? In addition to getting clear on what the problem is, defining the problem also establishes a goal for what you want to achieve.

2. Generate Alternate Solutions

- Brainstorm the idea
- Understand Common Interest
- Identify possible solutions

Input: What are some ways to solve the problem?

This is a critical step that is usually missing. Interests are the needs that you want satisfied by any given solution. We often ignore our true interests as we become attached to one particular solution. The best solution is the one that satisfies everyone's interests.

3. Evaluate and select an Alternative

Input: What can be done to solve the problem; decision-making criteria

The ideal solution to be effective or not (it will meet the goal), efficient (is affordable), and has the fewest side effects (limited consequences from implementation).

4. Implement the Solution

Input: Decision; planning; hard work

The implementation of a solution requires planning and execution.

5. Review and Measure the Output

Input: Resolutions; results of the implementation.

Leaders may be called upon to order the solution to be implemented by others, "sell" the solution to others or facilitate the implementation by involving the efforts of others. The most effective approach, by far, has been to involve others in the implementation to minimize resistance.

Role of Critical Thinking to Solve Problems

The quote by Jean De La Bruyere: "Life is a tragedy for those who feel, and a comedy for those who think," may seem a bit radical, however, according to the premise of cognitive psychology, what you think is what you feel.

- While many people believe that your feelings precede, or are independent of your thoughts, the truth is that your feelings are products of your thoughts.
- This revelation can be both daunting and liberating.
- Daunting because it makes us responsible for our attitudes and liberating because we have the power to choose our perspective, mood and thoughts.
- When we are aware that we can choose and direct our thinking, we realize that we have the ability to better control the circumstances of our lives, improve our decision-making processes and generally live more productive lives.
- This in no way suggests that we need downplay the many feelings and emotions we as humans enjoy, it's a simply a way for us to manage and balance them with our cognitive abilities.
- Every problem we are able to resolve increases self-confidence and self-worth.

Critical Thinking **helps to handle difficult challenges, more skillfully.** It is an amazing skill to develop and greatly improve your capacity to make objective, effective choices and arguments.

"Patience and perseverance have a magical effect

Before which difficulties disappear

And obstacles vanish"

—John Quincy Adams

Chapter 7

Exceed the Expectations by Raising the Performance Bar

Most of us work so hard every day.......doing all we can to succeed, be productive, excel in life, be a good employee or employer, be a good parent, Mom or Dad, son or daughter, etc.

Do you feel appreciated?

How often do you feel appreciated?

Isn't it amazing when someone does something so unexpected that makes you realize YOU are appreciated!?!

Exceeding the Expectation can be done with Performance Excellence. Performance excellence refers to an integrated approach to performance against expected goals, which one is expected to meet or exceed.

Don't lower your expectations to meet your performance. Raise your level of performance to meet your expectations. Expect the best of yourself, and then do what is necessary to make it a reality. Ralph Marston

There are 3 Steps for Exceeding the Expectation

Step 1. Define the Outcome

If you have higher aspirations or an outcome for yourself, then you cannot compare yourself to the masses. You must instead look at ways you can separate yourself from the masses. However, having said that, making comparisons with others is rarely helpful.

- What do I want to achieve?
- What are my objectives, short term and long term ?
- Who do I seek to become as a result of achieving this goal?
- What traits would I need to cultivate to achieve this goal?
- What new behaviors would I need to adopt?
- How would I ideally like to live my life having achieved this goal?

Step 2. Under commit: Pay attention- every small details matter

Small things really do matter if do we stay calm and do not over commit

- I will try to accomplish
- Not sure if I can do this
- Looks difficult but will try
- This may need a lot of time and or resources
- Not an easy task but will try
- Developing risk based assumptions

Step 3. Over perform: Make Outstanding things Happen

Challenge yourself by significantly raising your personal standards while building supportive rituals. Then go all-out by doing all you possibly can to reach those lofty standards. It of course might not work out, but there is also a chance it may provide ways to move things forward in a better way. However, without having taken that risk, you will never really know what you're truly capable of.

- Whew, this beats the goals
- Wow, done it well
- Excellent performance
- Outstanding performance

Finding the Motivation to Change

"Progress is impossible without change, and those who cannot change their minds cannot change anything" George Bernard Shaw

You probably acknowledge now that the personal standards you keep determine the expectations you set; determine the quality of your results, and the overall quality of your life. Even if you have high aspirations and big goals, living with a low set of standards will prevent you from ever reaching them. So something must change. YOU must change.

When it comes to change, there comes a point in everyone's life when enough is enough. *You suddenly recognize that you are fed-up with how your life is at* *the moment and you are determined to make a change for the better. In fact, you just can't bear another day with sub-standard results.*

The fact that you have finally acknowledged that something must change is an important first step. However, the process of change may not be easy. You will need the necessary leverage to make this change successfully.

Every great dream begins with a dreamer. Always remember, you have within you the strength, the patience, and the passion to reach for the stars to change the world. Harriet Tubman.

4 Step process to Raise your Performance Bar

To raise the standards of quality, that is set as benchmark.

It is 4 Step Process:

4.1. Plan or Set up the benchmark or Performance Standards

It's important at this stage not to see your goal from the limited perspective of your current reality. Instead, envision your goal from the future perspective of your desired reality.

- What could I potentially achieve if I had no limitations?
- What would be the possibilities?
- What can be the changes made
- What is the level on minimum outcome standards?

4.2. Evaluate the Performance

Here you analyze the current and desired reality. Your current reality is the life you are living at this very moment. Consider what kind of life this really is and the types of behaviors that define your actions and results in the present moment.

- What standards do I currently live by?
- What standards do I have for myself in various situations?
- What behaviors and actions do I partake in within these situations?
- What standards do I have for the roles I play in my life?

4.3. Exceed the Performance vs Benchmark

When it comes to raising your personal standards and making them stick for the long-haul, you must be willing to create small rituals that will help you meet these new expectations.

- Make outstanding things happen
- Reduce a big plan to several smaller plans
- Create something new and beyond expectations

Small unnoticed accomplishments become bigger success.

An ounce of performance is worth pounds of promises. Mae West

4.4. Raise the Initial Benchmark or Previous Performance Standards by Center of Excellence

Consider your goals and the roles you play. Now honestly ask yourself whether or not you are doing your very best in all these areas of your life.

- Can this be further Improved?
- Learn from mistakes….To err is human
- Where could I potentially do better?
- What standards can be set higher?
- When can we have higher goals?
- Why we cannot improve …what it will take to do better?
- Can we improve efficiency?
- Can we Improve effectiveness?

Center of Excellence is a continuous improvement where the standard or performance continuously gets better for higher output or for a higher target better than before. It is designed to raise the performance, to exceed in potential and the higher objectives of performance.

"Is it not strange that desire should so many years outlive performance?" William Shakespeare

Performing at your very best will always ensure that you are improving and moving forward, as long as you learn from every experience and use those lessons to improve on your past performances, it will lead YOU TO SUCCESS when you follow success attributes.

Some attributes of Excellence beyond Expectations: Your attitude matters in achieving high accomplishments.

- I do not accept mediocrity...
- I am the best and will even get better..
- I will not be ordinary or average...
- I do not get complacent, I am level headed..
- I know I can do better, and I will do better...
- I will not settle for less than my very best...

Achievement drive means having high personal and professional standards. It means striving to improve and meet new, higher standards of excellence. It gives a person a rewarding career, a sense of accomplishment and recognition from peers.

Continuous success in efforts leads to job promotion and all-round mental growth and development with better quality of life and growth of Positive Attitude towards Achievement and Center of Excellence in life.

The stronger your faith is, the greater the expectation is - the miracles follow. Faith becomes Is the Birthplace for Miracles and the Heart of Expectancy

Learn to appreciate your life, and excel in what you can achieve.

"There is more to life than increasing its speed.

So stop running so fast. Slow down a little bit.

Learn how to breathe. Feel your pulse, your heart beat.

Feel the life and the energy that runs through you.

Feel the life in your life"

—Mahatma Gandhi

Chapter 8

Radiate by Sustained Individual Brilliance

"If I'm working as an engineer for another band, the responsibility for brilliance pretty much rests on their shoulders. I think I'm pretty good, but I'm not good enough to turn a trout into a sausage, or the other way around" Steve Albini

Every man is equal in the crowd, unless his head is noticed by a leader.

Given the opportunity to lead, is an honor and one should make best out of it.

Dial a Life Line

If you're a junior member of a team, others may look to you as the default option for picking up miscellaneous duties. It's also not uncommon for senior associates (who aren't really supposed to be in the position of assigning you work anyway) to try and put projects on your plate. And these types of requests can be tricky to navigate or turn down.

If you're feeling pressure from senior team members or other leaders or departments, mention that, given your current priorities, you'll have to check with your manager. Then, go back and talk to your boss about the request, and you can decide how to handle it together.

Grab thy opportunity, when it presents itself

In most jobs, there will be situations where you're asked to take on extra tasks or assist in areas outside of your traditional role. Sometimes; this can be good exposure and a great way to build relationships with new people and teams. And other times, you may wonder why on earth you went to college, if this is what's become of your career.

Farmers understand the value of doing the job when they prepare the soil and plant their seeds in the ground. All of this work must be done at the correct time of the year and without compensation of any kind. If the farmer does his job correctly, he can count on Mother Nature to reward his hard work with a hundredfold return. This natural law of increasing returns works exactly the same for salespeople who go the extra mile providing service for their customers as it does for the farmer planting his crop.

"By creating a context of pressure, I can exact more preciseness, more brilliance. It's just as if coal is subjected to enormous pressure, you can   get a diamond"
John McLaughlin

Watch out for "Once in a lifetime Opportunity"

Salient opportunities do come by; they give us butterflies in our stomachs. They feel as though, if we play our cards just right, we will go places and experience things that we couldn't otherwise.

Thus, we feel compelled to say yes to: that job, that project, this risk, that trip, that guy/girl, that client, etc. ... all because they are "once-in- a-lifetime opportunities".

After we say yes, we enter into these situations with an incredible amount of pressure. We tell ourselves, "You'd better make this count!" Or "If you screw this up, there's no recovery!" But who can perform well under that kind of pressure? And if (heaven forbid) it doesn't work out; there can be all kinds of regret about missing out, losing out, or messing things up. After all, it's called an "once-in-a-lifetime opportunity" because it only happens once, right?

Well, here's the deal: That "once-in-a-lifetime opportunity" is not what we tend to think it is. I'm learning more and more that life doesn't work like that.

Sure (don't get me wrong), there certainly are opportunities that are incredibly unique and distinct in their particular flavor; there may not ever be another other like it.

But when we talk about "once-in-a-lifetime" it is often in a fatalistic and singular way, as if it's the only way to get from point A to point B. We think that between where we are and what we want to go is a chasm which only this "once-in-a-lifetime" opportunity bridges.

The "once-in-a-lifetime" event at hand, whatever it may be, is only one of many ways across. It may be the most obvious, most present, and the most appealing right now, but it's almost certainly not the only way to get where we want to go.

So take the risk when it makes sense. If it doesn't work out, know that (as the saying goes), "there's more than one way to skin a cat." (Gross, but true.)

If the Opportunity is not there, then Create it

"If opportunity doesn't knock, build a doo" Milton Berle

Opportunities are missed by most people, because they don't realize they've encountered such.

Here is one of those basic laws in life: There will always be opportunities for those who recognize and pursue them.

The lucky people are simply those who have taken more chances than average.

Why Wait for the Opportunity…. Create your own Opportunities

- *Know your limits.* – You can't be perfect. You can't do everything yourself. You can't create a business or live the life of your dreams or make a lot of money if you don't know your weaknesses, strengths and passions. If you know your limits and what you are capable of, you will know exactly what you need. Once you begin to know yourself, you will realize your weakness and you can fill these weaknesses with others people's strengths.
- *Open your eyes.* – There is a lot more happening in the world than you see. Stop listening to music all the time you are riding the bus or the train. Maybe there is someone who can change your life in that bus/train. Maybe the person sitting next to you is your next business partner or your husband/wife or your new best friend. You just never know, life is unpredictable, and that's why you should always keep your eyes wide open. You might miss an opportunity simply because you were too busy listening to your iPod. Always be on the lookout even when doing simple activities as drinking coffee, riding the bus or walking back home.
- *Meet new people.* – If you want to be presented with more opportunities, simply meet new people. The more people you know, the higher chances you will be presented with new experiences. Go to meetings with people having similar interests as you. Visit conferences.

You can even meet people online these days; join different Facebook groups, follow people on twitter; join LinkedIn. People are not as mean as you think. Also if you are one of those people who meet a lot of people on a daily basis and have a problem remembering their names this app will help you a lot – Anki (This app will make you never forget a name, job position or age again. It does miracles.)

- **Don't be afraid to ask.** – Just DON'T! There is no shame in not knowing something, and there is no shame in questioning things. Do you know how I got my first job? I simply asked the manager if I could work here and, after he interrogated me a bi, he said; "Yes". So I found a job by simply asking a question in a company that wasn't looking for employees. Most people would gladly help you if you asked them nicely for some help. People are not monsters; most of us are good and kind. You just have to ask the right way.

- **Don't be afraid to try a different approach.** – In Bulgaria blogging is not something people make money out of.
  Story of a successful Blogger: Here most people don't even know what blogging is and when I decided I wanted to blog, people laughed at me and told me to find myself a serious job. But I didn't think so; I knew I could create a successful blog myself and that all happened, thanks to the steps I mentioned above. And in the end I did. Now I am earning fiv times more than what my friends are earning. I am working from home I work when I want to and I haven't even mentioned the best thing yet – I am doing something meaningful; I am helping people and I love that I simply love what I do. Why? Because I wasn't afraid to go out of the box. Just because the masses of people think something is wrong, doesn't mean they are right.
  Try New Approach, where no one walks you walk like a King.

- **Travel.** – You should visit different places at least one time a year. This way you will surely meet new people and also might be presented with an opportunity that simply doesn't exist at your hometown. A friend of mine went for a vacation at Montreal, but he never came back. He found a job there and he liked it so much that he decided to stay in Montreal. If a land is explored it may be even better than dark hole.

- **Build self-confidence.** – You can't make people follow you if you don't look confident. That's why you need confidence; you need to be sure 120% that things will work out right in the end if you want other people to believe you as well. It might be fake confidence, but you need to hav it. Most people follow the leaders even when they make bad decisions simply because of their leadership status. And if you could make people follow you, you will surely be able to create a lot of opportunities for yourself/ your company/ your work place.

- *Keep learning.* – Learning is a process that never ends. You can always learn something new. Always maintain the attitude of student. If you think you are finished learning, bitterness set in, but if you have more to achieve every day, that makes each morning's awakening full of potential.
- *In the end it all comes to doing.* You will never get presented with opportunities by sitting and watching TV all day. Go out, feel, see, be and take part of active life. If you are active and always on the lookout you will always end up on the right place in the right moment.

"We see opportunities as opportunities only when we are ready to see them, otherwise we see them as difficulties"– Hristiqn Nikolov

Reflections on "How I created Niche Industrial Products to gain huge Competitive advantage"

Whenever there is a problem, there has to be Solution.

If we look it as opportunity to solve the problem, we can have an advantage of becoming leaders and gaining huge competitive advantage.

Recall my good corporate stint in India where I worked with the Hilton Group, an Industrial Rubber Conveyor Belting Manufacturing company. The product Belting sold to the Industrial Core Sector was very technical and expensive. It was often customized to the buyer's requirement. This product had extensive usage in the Primary Core sector Industry which involved Thermal Power Plants, Cement Industry, Mining, Steel Plants, Port Trusts, Shipyards, Fertilizer and Chemical companies. The product involved extensive technical design to meet the material handling load requirements.

Problem vs Creative Solution

The Belting product was expensive and each order was in large quantity running into 1000 meters and above and is worth a large amount of money. Each customer was very selective and performed several rounds of Technical and

Financial negotiation before finalizing the order. It was not easy market condition and was more challenging with the presence of large multinationals and intensive price wars. It was a very competitive buyers' market.

In the Thermal Sector one of the problem areas that I noticed was that the belting had a short life due to its usage as it was carrying coal-hot burning material. The coal was carried over a large distance during the manufacturing and mining process. Typically the average belt life was only 6 to 8 months. This was a huge problem area and buyers suffered large costs of product replacement.

How I took upon this challenge for the First time in the country to come up with Creative Reengineering, to create something new for this solution.

With the help of Technical Expert Mr. Vijay Gupta, Tech guru of Conveyor Belting, we visited the Thermal Power Plants and performed extensive study for product analysis. We took upon the challenge of creating a customized *Heat Resistant Belting*. The industrial product specifications were not geared to meet high heat resistance and hence resulting in the low life of the product.

We had to go back to the drawing board and start from basic.

It was an extensive effort against all odds to reengineer the product, **but it was a Creative Solution that changed the face of the Industry**.

So we went thought the pains to re re-engineer the belting and came up with a totally new product design. But then we had some other challenges. We found that we had to import the higher tensile fabric, as it was not available in the domestic market, and also import special raw materials for meeting new product requirements. We approached our company management to import desired products which was a sustained effort, but *we were able to convince the Creative Solution approach* vs Cost Benefit Analysis.

Then we worked closely with our technical staff in the manufacturing plant. We did experience a lot of resistance, as there was a lot of waste.

Extensive efforts were required to try new things and produce extra ordinary quality. The experiments were expensive and arduous. Not an easy task.

The entire process required grit, determination and a positive attitude.

Finally we were able to produce the product and delivered it to the customer for trials. The quality of Heat Resistant Conveyor Belting turned out to be great. The customer was happy with the trial order and ordered a large quantity with repetitive business. It was a huge success for our efforts, against odds.

With this success story we approached other thermal power plants and also customized the product. This product became exclusive and we led from the front. We collected huge orders and, both market share and profitability greatly improved.

Thus we created a Niche product tailored for the Thermal sector, a massive breakthrough in the Industry!

Likewise we performed a similar feat in the fertilizer Industry. We approached a large fertilizer factory. Here we created a customized *Chemical Resistant Belting* for them to carry the fertilizers. Likewise the customer was happy, as the product performance turned out to be great. Then we approached other fertilizers units in the country, a*nother massive breakthrough in the Industry.*

We built a Niche product for the Fertilizer industry and obtained a huge competitive advantage. The product became exclusive and we were able to sell with huge margins as market Leaders.

These both the success stories reflect on creating a solution when we face the problem. The results of efforts are always rewarding.

Radiate by your sustained Individual Brilliance: By going the Extra mile.

One can carry his individual brilliance and lead others, radiate and leave an impact of sustained efforts, covering the extra mile, being an outstanding team member is to lead from front.

Going the extra mile is outstanding or individual brilliance is reflected by the following virtues:

- Make an extra effort...go the extra mile
- Try very hard to achieve something different

Radiate by Sustained Individual Brilliance

- Try the spirit of adventure
- Do more than expected
- Make special efforts
- Perform inventory of your strengths and weakness
- Be Proactive and lead from the front
- Don't wait for permission to do more
- Manage your own interest/bottom-up approach

Other examples of "Going the extra mile" can be enumerated as follows:

- When it comes to weaker students, the teacher goes the extra mile to help them understand.
- It is often required to go the extra mile in order to come up new Ideas and benefit customers.
- I love staying at that hotel. They go the extra mile to make their guests happy.
- She is a very nice person and is always willing to go the extra mile to help others.
- If you are willing to go the extra mile at work, you are bound to get noticed and grow professionally.
- I was impressed with the way the customer service officer went the extra mile to resolve my problem.
- It is often required to go the extra mile in order to keep a relationship strong and happy.
- He's not a very loyal person. I wouldn't go the extra mile to keep him in our team.
- Team captain goes an extra mile to train and coach weaker members so that the team succeeds
- Fire Fighter went an extra mile to rescue trapped victim in burning debris and saved his life

"And whosoever shall compel thee to go a mile, go with him twain."

Under the Roman Impressment Law, a Roman soldier passing by a Jew could order him to carry his pack for one mile.

Jesus asked his followers "Go two miles instead of one"

(This phrase is an adaptation of a commandment of Jesus in the Sermon of Mount (Matthew Ch 5 v 41)

Chapter 9

Outperform the Tasks by Principles of

Center of Excellence

A performance task is any learning activity or assessment that one is asked to perform to demonstrate their knowledge, understanding and proficiency.

"To achieve something that you've never achieved before, you must become someone that you have never been before." Motivational speaker Les Brown.

When someone outperforms the tasks he has exceeded the performance expectations. But not all do all the time, so let's examine some issues and factors that influences our performance:

- Have you committed to personal excellence?

- Are we recognized for Outstanding Performance?

- Do you strive toward it, but find obstacles in your way that leave you short of your goal?

- What are various constraints that affect your performance?

As human we all have bounded rationality and influenced by 5 elements, that deeply impact our societal co-existence, value and beliefs.

5 Elements that deeply influence your daily life

- Physical
- Emotional
- Social
- Family
- Spiritual

Physical: Our lifestyle and daily activities. Performing and excelling in physical activities that require aerobic fitness, endurance, strength, healthy body composition and flexibility derived through exercise, nutrition and training.

Emotional: We live with an emotional state. Approaching life's challenges in a positive, optimistic way by demonstrating self-control, stamina and good character with your choices and actions, are factors in your success.

Social: We make choices. Developing and maintaining trusted, valued relationships and friendships that are personally fulfilling and fostering good communication including a comfortable exchange of ideas, views, and experiences, all add to the positive social mass we cherish.

Family: We are family oriented. Being part of a family unit that is safe, supportive and loving, and provides the resources needed for all members to live in a healthy and secure environment.

Spiritual: We are spiritual by inner strengths. One's purpose, core values, beliefs, identity and life vision. These elements, which define the essence of a person, enable one to build inner strength, make meaning of experiences, behave ethically, persevere through challenges, and be resilient when faced wit adversity.

An individual's spirituality draws upon personal, philosophical, psychological, and/or religious teachings, and forms the basis of their character.

You may need to understand them, balance your behavior and actions by positives that gives you strength to attain the Center of excellence in your life.

Key factors influencing Performance/Make Outstanding Things Happen

There are many factors in our lives that make us keep going and keep evolving, getting better as we go along. However when we are on track to outperform and achieve faster results, there are many factors which influence the outcome of outstanding performance.

- **Goal setting**: Goal setting is an important process; it gives life a sense of direction. Without Goal setting we have no targets to achieve and no motivation to accomplishment something.

Goals are what take us forward in life; they are the oxygen to our dreams. They are the first steps to every journey we take and are also our last. It's very important that you realize the significance and importance of goal-setting and apply this knowledge in your life. Begin with the end in mind. - Stephen Covey.

- **Development of Practical skills:** It is said that only 10 percent of adult learning happens in the classroom, from books, tapes, or online learning activities. 70 % comes by doing, and the balance (20%) comes from what we keep doing. So we need to DO things/take action and get involved.

- **Identify what you Love to do**: You may already know the answer to this, but you might not have committed it to paper or put together an action plan to turn what you love to do into your full-time career.

Maybe you'd like to write a screenplay for a blockbuster movie ...write the perfect spy novel ... become the world's best white paper writer, or perhaps what you're doing now is exactly what you want to be doing. Finding something you love to do is so vitally important, "Many people make more progress in a couple of years doing something they love and suits their talents than working 20 years at a job that is not a good fit that they really don't enjoy."

- **Practice, Practice, and more Practice** – No matter what you want to do in your career, there is no substitute for actually practicing your craft. The more you practice, the more competent and skilled you'll become. And the faster you'll start to experience all the benefits of being a master at your craft.

- **Time Management**; Respect time and organize the activities with careful attention. *Time and a bullet behave similarly, once gone it never comes back.*

- **Continuous Improvement**: Keep a laser-like focus on the skills you'll need in the future – What additional skills, knowledge and information will you need to be a leader in your marketplace in the months and years ahead? You should always be projecting yourself three to five years into the future.

- **Education:** Determine what you need to be studying. Plan for both now and down the road so you'll be, if not the best, one of the best paid people in your industry.

Attributes for Visionary Leadership/ Your Extraordinary Excellences

Visionary leaders see the untapped potential in their teams. These leaders focus on communication, organization, charisma, and strategic thinking with sense of urgency.

- o **Communication** – You need to be able to visualize and communicate the goals of the project and the dreams you have for your team. Only then can you engage in a meaningful dialogue with the team to learn about their dreams and establish 'how' the TEAM will complete the project's goals.
- o **Charisma** – Enthusiasm is an important emotion that you, as the belt, need to display and demonstrate as you lead your team. Genuine enthusiasm and encouragement can positively influence your team members and improve their engagement.
- o **Organization** – Your organizational skills start when you are first read the project's business case and objectives. Organizing your thoughts and potential approach to the project will lead you to the knowledge and skills that your team will need. Once the knowledge and skills have been identified you need to take the time to build your teams. Can you select and organize people in a way that allows their best skills and talents to shine?
- o **Strategic Thinking** – Can you strategize what the real vision for the team will be? You need to be able to look to the future and see where everyone will fit and how you will run the project. Predict where you think the DMAIC process will lead you, what your team can achieve and communicate a tactical plan to achieve success. You can and will need to push your team in a positive manner.

- ○ **Sense of urgency:** One needs to value the sense of urgency to get things done. To be Outstanding performer, the race starts begins right away. The time to commit to becoming one of the top performers is NOW.

The Time Starts NOW. ….Not tomorrow or the next day.

It's Today……RIGHT NOW.

Committing on Center of Excellence, is a life of positives

Committing to Center of Excellence helps in identifying areas in your life that need to be developed and consequently developing these areas to the best of your ability. It's about integrating them into your everyday living.

 It's about creating positive, enjoyable and worthwhile habits that propel you towards your goal. The benefit is that you become a greater individual. *The journey to excellence becomes enjoyable. It helps you gain that edge.*

- Care more than others think is wise
- Dream bigger than others think is practical
- Expect more than others think is possible
- Risk more than others think is safe
- Do not accept half-hearted results
- And remember, it starts with YOU and ends with YOU
- Raise the benchmark after having achieved the performance bar
- Continuously improve and improve your Skills, Attitude and Beliefs

With these 5 elements that surround you on daily basis, **learn and adopt Key Factors influencing Outperformance/Make Outstanding Things Happen**, you will be able to set your eyes as to on How to accomplish Center of Excellence, you will surely be able to find a Success story with your Tasks, Performances and Accomplishments.

And then you will transform into a person with Extra Ordinary abilities.

"Winners are ordinary people with

Extraordinary determination"

- Lincoln

Center of Excellence set-up in a Business Framework

A Center of Excellence (CoE), in Business Language is not a myth or a broken dream, **but is also known as a Competency center or a Capability center in a successful Organization.**

This is where as a corporate group or a team, leads other employees and the organization as a whole, in some particular area of focus such as a skill, best practices, technology, lean behavior or discipline

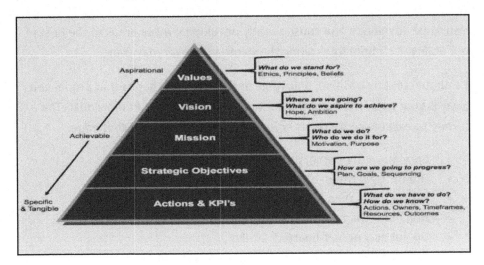

A Strategic COE needs to be set-up for Organized Success

COE in handling Strategic Vision, Functional and Guiding Principles:

- **BPM/Process Improvement** – This is the most strategic of all CoEs since all businesses are made up of processes. We see a few companies establish this as a CoE. and also create a role for a 'Global Business Improvement Executive'. It allows for all the traditional focus of lean and six sigma as well as for creating new strategies and business capabilities.
- **Project Management Office (PMO)** – Many fail to think of themselves as a CoE and act as little more than a governance body, but the most successful PMOs grow beyond that single focus and take on a full CoE role around Program-Project management. This has evolved and some successful organization has set it up for Organization Excellence, a

culture of refinement and Best Practices. These organizations are bound to succeed due to good attitude and stay ahead of the competition.

- **Lean Six Sigma** – Perhaps six sigma is the most mature of the CoEs that some organizations have embraced. This type of CoE was invented by Motorola and popularized by GE. Many companies have grown this into a strategic asset they use to differentiate them and drive competitiveness. It has formal roles (Champions, Sponsors, and Black Belts); a well understood methodology (DMAIC), standard set of tools (Statistical Process Control (SPC), etc.), a formal certification process (Green Belt, Black Belt, Master Black Belt) and an active community.
- **ITIL Framework**. It is a great framework of Standard Process and Practices which allows companies to have Best Practices and a Continuous Improvement model. I have seen that without an ITIL process, rules are haphazard and unrefined. You succeed to fail or follow the hard path of gruesome learning curve.
- **Quality Assurance CoE**– Whether for new product or software development, the complexity of the roles, tools and techniques needed for quality often get formalized into a CoE. This may be tied to a six sigma CoE or stand alone for complex QA Matrices and Better Quality standards Framework.
- **Business Analysis** – Some organizations have embraced the idea that getting business requirements, especially around software development, are a problem best addressed by a Coe. A certification for Business Analysts from the IIBA has further advanced this idea.
- **Communications** – Corporate communications, employee and customer relations are activities that are often supported by a centralized support process or function. At a basic level, their role is to support the line business around this focus area.
- **Risk and Compliance** – Many organizations have created this capability without formally calling it a CoE. Insurance and financial institutions without exception will have this function. Other verticals may also embrace it. They almost always have veto power on changes to business processes or external communications. In ideal cases, they will help deploy   standards and facilitate understanding throughout the organization.
- **Human Resources** – Another "function" or support process many businesses have embraced at a strategic level that meets the definition of a CoE. HR-IS has become a complex standards of Excellence when

large resources over 10,000 to 100,000 employees are evaluated for Performance, Growth and Excellence at workplace.

All of this has a great result when there is Strategic Vision within an organization. Individuals are treated as assets and, the process and systems are continuously improved. That is evolved by continuous Improvement, organized practices and an attitude towards lean improvement

Center of Excellence strategically influences the main processes within an organization, that complement the line businesses. *It Plans and Promotes Organizational Competency and Excellences across the width and depth of organizational structure with Common Corporate Vision and Goals.*

Stephen Jenner and Craig Kilford, in Management of Portfolios, mentions that Center of Excellence is a coordinating function which ensures that change initiatives are delivered consistently and well, through standard processes and competent staff.

- Responsibilities: Center of Excellence Division: Serves 5 Basic Organizational Needs
- Support: For their area of focus, CoE's should offer support to the business lines. This may be through services needed, or providing subject matter experts.
- Guidance: Standards, methodologies, tools and knowledge repositories are typical approaches to filling this need.
- Shared Learning: Training and certifications, skill assessments, team building and formalized roles are all ways to encourage shared learning
- Measurements: CoEs should be able to demonstrate they are delivering the valued results that justified their creation through the use of output metrics.
- Governance: Allocating limited resources (money, people, etc.) across a their possible use is an important function of CoEs. They should ensure organizations invest in the most valuable projects and create economies of scale for their service offering. In addition, coordination across other corporate interests is needed to enable the CoE to deliver value.

Center of Excellence framework makes treating an employee as an asset, grows a company's inherent Product Quality, leads to better trained employees, higher employee retention, and generates good work ethics and the profitability in the market place.

"Center of Excellence gives Organizations - An Edge in the Market place". It Builds a Critical Mass of successful Strategy and Comradeship.

Not all organizations have embraced CoE, due to limitation of their leadership strategy and planning, thereby having challenges of attrition, high employee turnover and limitations of growth.

However many organizations who have adapted successfully have accomplished great results in the areas of Strategic Success, Higher employee Retention and Leadership in the Market place.

Center of Excellence speaks of successful dynamism and growth.

The critical issue when it comes to COEs isn't whether the work they're doing is important to the business. It is how to ensure that their effort isn't wasted.

Center of Excellence makes the synergy of best minds, strategically achieving common objectives, for the success of an organization.

"The happy life is thought to be one of excellence;

now an excellent life

requires exertion,

and does not consist in amusement".

—Aristotle

Chapter 10

Lead into 21st Century by Analytics/Business Intelligence COE

Gartner Says "Worldwide Business Intelligence and Analytics Market to reach $22.8 Billion in 2017 growing exponentially at @ 3000 to 5000 % in next 3 to 5 years"

Recent speech by Mark Berger, Gartner Research Director at a recent BI summit at Chicago, mentioned that 90% of the companies are already lagging behind in their thinking and skills of the future worker.

Let's face it the Leadership is challenged. Individuals have to adapt to growing data-intensive consumer-centric behavior analytics for success of consumer products by predictive behavior.

Research has called customer experience the ultimate competitive advantage and companies are creating new tools to help businesses monitor and manage it effectively. It's clear that customer experience is increasingly important to organizations around the globe, but what does it really mean?

Customer experience feels like a buzzword that you could easily swap out for "customer service" or other more tangible concepts, but it's actually much larger. Individuals as well as Corporate Strategy will revolve around Consumer Centric Demand Management and whole Dynamics of Business Intelligence.

21st Century challenge is huge- both for Corporate and Individuals

Corporate have to take Strategic stride to gain market share and Individuals have to sharpen the skills to be more competitive.

Researches show that most of the organizations are just beginning their BI journey and faced with the fundamental question of where to begin!

Peter Senge in his book The Fifth Discipline has mentioned that the business conditions have become so tough that, if you risk people's ire you will make yourself vulnerable. Leadership is no longer a personal mastery but needs suitable business tools and mental models, shared vision and team learning to deliver results.

- Modern BI at scale will dominate new buying — while business users initially flocked to new modern tools because they could be used without IT assistance, the increased need for governance will serve as the catalyst for renewed IT engagement. Modern BI tools that support greater accessibility, agility and analytical insight at the enterprise level will dominate new purchases.
- New innovative and established vendors will drive the next wave of market disruption — The emergence of smart data discovery capabilities, machine learning and automation of the entire analytics workflow will drive a new flurry of buying because of its potential value to reduce time to insights from advanced analytics and deliver them to a broader set of people across the enterprise. While this "smart" wave is being driven by new innovative startups, traditional BI vendors that were slow to adjust to the current "modern" wave are driving it in some cases.
- Need for complex datasets drives investments in data preparation — business users want to analyze a diverse, often large and more complex combinations of data sources and data models, faster than ever before. The ability to rapidly prepare, clean, enriches and finds trusted datasets in a more automated way becomes an important enabler of expanded use.
- Extensibility and embed ability will be key drivers of expanded use and value. Both internal users and customers will either use more automated tools or will embed analytics, in the applications they use in their context, or a combination of both. The ability to embed and extend analytics content will be a key enabler of more pervasive adoption and value from analytics.

- Support for real-time events and streaming data will expand use. Organizations will increasingly leverage streaming data generated by devices, sensors and people to make faster decisions. Vendors need to invest in similar capabilities to offer buyers a single platform that combines real-time events and streaming data with other types of source data.
- Interest in cloud deployments will continue to grow- Cloud deployments of BI and analytics platforms have the potential to reduce cost of ownership and speed time to deployment. However, data gravity that still tilts to the majority of enterprise data residing on-premises continues to be a major inhibitor to adoption. That reticence is abating and Gartner expects the majority of new licensing buying likely to be for cloud deployments by 2020.
- Marketplaces will create new opportunities for organizations to buy and sell analytic capabilities and speed time to insight-The availability of an active marketplace where buyers and sellers converge to exchange analytic applications, aggregated data sources, custom visualizations and algorithms is likely to generate increased interest in the BI and analytics space and fuel its future growth.

Business Intelligence Center of Excellence: BI COE or Analytics COE

BI COE, often called Analytics CoE, Big Data CoE, or Integration CoE, is an organizing mechanism to align People, Process, Technology, and Culture. The target benefits include: Better collaboration between Business and IT. Increased adoption and use of BI and Analytics is likely the order of the day.

Gartner Says Business Intelligence and Analytics Leaders Must Focus on Mindsets and Culture, to Kick Start Advanced Analytics.

Every day the business conditions are getting tougher, with new Corporate Laws of Governance, rapid Socio- Economic changes, political complexities, rapid globalization of trade and commerce, outsourcing etc., challenges are bigger.

David L Bradford in his book Leadership Wheel - Managing for Excellence, had mentioned that today Leadership needs to step in guiding developing high performances in contemporary Organizations.

The Business Intelligence Quadrant

B I Quadrant has been drawn based on Demand Management vs Supply Management and Industry Transformation of Business Intelligence:

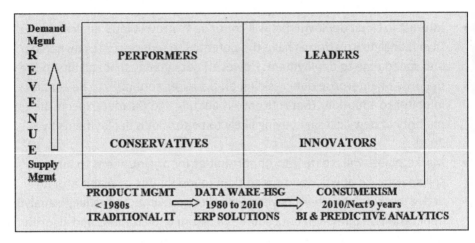

Looking at the trends in the last 35 years and emergence of Business Intelligenc Era has been an amazing evolution:

BI Leaders: Leaders have emerged when they have managed Demand Cycles ar kept abreast of Business Intelligence Analytics & Applications, to reach highest efficiency and dominance in market place. Examples being IoT, Media, Amazon, E-Commerce led by Google etc.

Innovators: Have modernized their operations quickly, adapted the latest Business Intelligence techniques, and transformed them into fighting-fit and highly-efficient entities challenging big brothers. Examples being, Computers, Media Group, Supply Chain, Healthcare, Utilities, Aerospace etc. led by IBM, Apple, Cisco, Facebook, U tube, and Wal-Mart to name a few.

Performers: Are traditional Big brothers who have so far managed demand cycles but lack the spirit of innovation and B. I. adaptability. They are also under severe pressure to crumble and lose their profitability. Industry example being Automotive, Chemicals, Construction, Cement Manufacturing etc. Gener Motors, Ford, DuPont as examples.

Conservative: Have been traditionally Supply based entities who had a good run initially, but are now still needing traditional leadership approach with inadequate Tech and B I potency, are heading into oblivion. References can be Iron & Steel Industry, Forging units, Textiles etc.

Historically 2015 and 2016 saw Amazon's QuickSight and IBM's Watson Analytics Service enter the BI market, along with major enhancements from Microsoft to its Power BI suite, including a recent Cortana integration. Oracle and SAP have been in the market for years; and will look to hit back against the newer players with significant investments in revamping their BI offerings.

2017 has bought major update from Google for its BigQuery BI platform, and who knows, maybe by 2020 some innovator will enter the fray and upstage the Goliaths. The interesting war has already started!

BI Attributes vs Center of Excellence

Paula L Rechner and Dan R Dalton in their book: CEO Duality and Organizational Performance - A Longitudinal Analysis, has mentioned that CEOs have to manage the unexpected, and in order to be a leader one has to adapt, otherwise they sink.

Sinking Raft Vs Floating Raft: Business Intelligence module is like a floating raft, example mentioned in Forbes magazine, where there were two groups of CEOs on two different rafts. One was asked to obey the policies, follow the production cycle, and follow a perceived path. They sank. However the other group, who was encouraged to proceed and were thought to be fit, seemed to be obviously enjoy themselves, and kept their raft floating.

Pull technology vs Push technology: Advent of Business Intelligence had proved that today we cannot have a technology which we use to survive (Push) but something which can take the business to the next level (Pull). It is the era of Data Analytics and BPM to outperform and outclass the competition.

Business Intelligence sparks business dynamism. One needs to be stay ahead of learning curve. If not, then leadership can get into trouble.

Business Intelligence provides visionary interface, where it exults leaders to managing the unexpected, lead from the front and stay ahead with technology.

To quote B.I. guru Mark Berger, "**By 2019 *B.I. style will be integrated into BPM and Data Analytics.* ***Over the last few years, new trends have emerged that have had an enormous influence on how organizations work, interact, communicate, collaborate and protect themselves***".

Eight IT 'meta-trends' that influences Organizations

These impacts strategies, operations and investments in a wide variety of ways:

1. Digitalization and Self-service BI
2. Consumerization and data quality/Master data management
3. Agility and Collaborative business intelligence accelerates insights
4. Security and Hyper Security/Data losses and Converging
5. Data Analytics. data discovery/visualization
6. Cloud and Machine Learning
7. Mobile technology/Internet of Things
8. Artificial Intelligence: Move from Reactive to Predictive

These meta-trends can be considered as the main drivers behind a number of important trends either, related to the usage of software and technologies for business intelligence/analytics and data management, or to the way BI is organized.

They generally shape the future of business intelligence and, more specifically, the BI and data management trends we analyzed.

For example, Sales departments have become more interested in data analysis with new uses of remote video monitoring and sales analysis along with customer data collection to create better shopping experiences. Customers will be the King. Business is becoming more and more customer-centric.

Advanced analytics will no longer be reserved for data scientists and experts.

Business users are already leveraging powerful analytics functions like k-means clustering and forecasting. With increasing size of data. hyper data threading is becoming normal. The formidable Forecasting is leading to Predictive Analysis. with customer insight, to predict future events.

7 Essential components for Analytics/BI Center of Excellence

According to several BI experts Individuals will play a big role in shaping the Center of Excellence.

1. Business users have greater success: Business Ownership over BI

Organizations that place BI in the hands of business users have greater success rates than those who confine BI within IT, Evelson says. This may mean embedding BI within lines of business or having BI operations report to the chief digital officer or chief customer officer.

"The business must absolutely be in charge," he adds.

Although the complexities of early BI technologies put IT in charge of many BI programs, today's tools are more intuitive, allowing them to go straight into the hands of business users who can run the queries that matter to them.

Similarly, the speed at which users need access to data and insights derived from BI has increased dramatically in recent years. Today's business users often need actionable information in real time and cannot wait for IT to generate reports.

As such, IT ownership can be an impediment, rather than an enabler, of BI success, Evelson says.

2. Business should own BI initiatives: Monitor BI use and adjust as necessary

Although the business should own BI initiatives, IT must remain an active partner in monitoring and evaluating the use of BI systems.

Evelson explains: "Rather than putting up roadblocks, monitor what they're doing, what data sources they're accessing, what tools they are using and how they are using them, whether the business unit A is using Business Intelligence more than business unit B."

In this way, he says, the CIO can set thresholds in partnership with business units. For instance, the CIO will know whether a few analysts in marketing have downloaded their own tool and are successfully using it, in which case it may be fine to leave them alone.

Likewise, the CIO will notice when that BI application has seen an increasing number of users across business and has thus become an enterprise-grade environment and a mission-critical enterprise app that requires additional discipline and governance, which will be pertinent for the success of the organization.

3. Validate, validate, and validate

Organizations may be tempted to quickly spin out lots of BI capabilities, but quality outweighs quantity, says Chris Hagans, Vice President of Operations for WCI Consulting, a consultancy focused on BI.

"It's better to have fewer things you trust than have a whole lot of things that are suspect," he says.

As a result, organizations need a strong validation process that focuses on enabling access to all the data needed to answer queries. It should also prevent problematic data from entering the BI system, so that it doesn't produce faulty insights. In addition, the validation process should be agile enough to respond quickly to requests for new BI functions.

Hagans points to a hypothetical use case in which a BI tool generates reports on net sales figures. If that tool takes in data on sales but doesn't figure in the number of sold items that are returned, then the end information is no good.

Moreover, Hagans says validation remains critical, not just to ensure accuracy, but also to head off skeptics.

"It only takes one or two people saying, 'I don't trust the data,' to invalidate a report. That can tank a whole project, and then reports just become worthless" he says.

4. Focus on Business problems first, then on Data

"Don't take a build-it-and-they-will-come approach to BI initiatives", Evelson warns. Too many organizations build data repositories, lay BI on top and then expect business users to jump right in and play, he says.

"What works much better is a top-down approach, one that's about business outcomes. We don't start with 'Where's the data?' We start with solving a business problem," he says.

Evelson lays out this example: Marketing spots a customer churn problem and wants to understand why customers are leaving. The organization should focus on delivering the capability to answer marketing's business question by first deciding what metrics need to be measured, accessing the data needed to calculate those metrics, and then enabling marketing to slice and dice the data.

"We need to identify a clear business problem first and what metrics we want to analyze, and then at the end of that we talk about where to get the data" says Evelson, a leading expert in business intelligence.

5. Prioritize and build BI strategy for both expansion and improvements

A successful BI strategy anticipates both expansion and improvements; according to BI leaders.

As such, organizations should know what business insights they want and which ones are most important so IT can deliver what's most critical to business users first and work its way through a priority list.

Moreover, the BI program should be able to shift as the priorities change.

"It has to evolve with what the users and the people inside the business community need," Hagans says.

Similarly, the BI strategy should build in processes to advance and improve how the system works. Evelson recommends an iterative approach, so that the BI tool can expand and improve as business units use it and determine where it meets their needs and where it doesn't.

5. Upskill 'citizen' data scientists

In its 2017 "Magic Quadrant for Business Intelligence and Analytics Platforms" report, research firm Gartner says "the number of citizen data scientists will grow five times faster than the number of data scientists" over the next several years. Data Analytics will transform the business needs.

Cindi Howson, a research Vice President at Gartner, mentioned that executives already recognize that there aren't enough data scientists to meet demand; they're also struggling to hire or identify in their existing ranks the citizen data scientists they'll need.

"We're talking about the in-between information analysts. They know the business domain and the questions to ask," she says, adding that there's a need for software that's easier to use so organizations can better enable these workers. Howson anticipates that software improvements will eventually allow businesspeople to ask and answer their own questions on un-modeled data set

As that happens, organizations will need the right people to take on this role of citizen data scientist. They'll need inquisitive workers with analytical skills who like to ask questions, know how to interpret the information they're getting back, and are comfortable using software to improve business outcomes.

7. Empower staff to tell stories with data

On a similar note, Todd Nash, President and Principal of CBIG Consulting, a professional services firm that helps clients leverage their data assets, says he has worked with organizations where workers understand how to use the insights offered by their BI tools to tell stories that help others understand "what the data is trying to say."

The data size will be Big Data. There will a lot of Data Mining and Analytics tool will emerge to give customer- friendly dashboards and Real Time Analysis.

"You have the data and the tools to tell the story, and you need people to marr those up," he says.

He says these people use the reporting and visualization functions built into BI technologies to develop narratives that help maximize the value of analytics.

This approach is not just about having people who produce slick-looking report Nash says these users are able to make connections with the data that others might not see, thereby offering new insights businesses can leverage for gains.

He says executives need to support and enable these workers as they explore those connections and present their insights.

For example, he says workers analyzing store sales figures might see how smaller weather trends — not just big storm events — have subtle impacts on sales. They might want to draw in external weather data to further analyze trends to better understand how the stores can optimize sales with this insight.

"There's all kind of internal and external data to take advantage of to get much better insights," Nash says, adding that successful BI programs allow analysts to move beyond measuring standard key performance indicators.

"There are just lots of different ways to challenge yourself," he says, "and part of that is challenging every KPI and making sure you're taking advantage of the information available to you to understand."

By 2019, Data analytics will become a mandatory core competency for professionals of all types. Much like proficiency in Microsoft Word, Excel, and PowerPoint, competency in analytics will gain prime considerations.

Big Data, Cloud services, Predictive analytics, and Data Science will continually innovating spaces that each feed into BI, huge role it plays within enterprises.

A business intelligence Center of excellence (BI CoE) thus helps a business gain deep insight into its products, services, customers and market initiatives, and consequently tweaks its strategies for maximum effectiveness.

Any Individual who adapts quickly and, gains new skills will be more successful in his lifetime. And a Leader who drives the Change will become futuristic, visionary and a succcssful Leader.

"Talent wins games,

But Teamwork and intelligence....Wins championships"

—Michael Jordan

(Greatest Basketball player of all times)

PART THREE

IMPLEMENT

CENTRE OF EXCELLENCE (COE)

ROADMAP

Chapter 11

Steps for Implementing Individual Center of Excellence

In the earlier chapters we have seen the importance of understanding your Halo to accomplish greatness in life, your Personality Traits, Mind power, Subconscious Mind, Creativity, Powers of Lateral Thinking to Create New Ideas and 6 Keys to Your Happiness, 12 Laws of Karma that will Change Your Life.

Individuals can Make Outstanding Things Happen:

Likewise we saw that you have a Powerful Potential and can create the Unexpected by Making Difficult things Possible, we can Exceed the Expectations by Raising the Bar, Radiate by Sustained Individual Brilliance, and we can Outperform the Tasks by following the Principles of Center of Excellence.

5 Step Process for Implementing Individual COE

These 5 Steps will help us to implement the COE and enhance our powerful Potential, follow the COE Roadmap as matrix of "How to Hit the Bull's Eye"

Step 1 Knowing Yourself
Step 2 Perform the SWOT Analysis
Step 3 Choosing your Life's decision wisely
Step 4 Doing things differently- Create Your Niche/Excellence
Step 5 Creating Center of Excellence – with Continuous Improvement

Step 1. Knowing Yourself

Gain knowledge about yourself

- Believe in Yourself
- Understand your Personality Traits
- Know your Mind Power and powerful Sub conscious Mind
- Assess your Creativity, Lateral Thinking vs Positive Attitude
- Understanding of Happiness as frame of Mind vs Karma as the Actions

This is an initial phase where we are learning about ourselves. We are trying to understand our abilities. We are trying to know our personality traits, our

Personality Patterns, inculcating belief in our own abilities, knowing our attitudes and mindset, subconscious awakening, creativity, lateral thinking etc.. If we can understand we have better chances of development and our Success.

Step 2. Perform the SWOT Analysis

Assess yourself vis-à-vis your surroundings. Know your 4 Key traits:

- Strengths
- Weakness
- Opportunity
- Threats

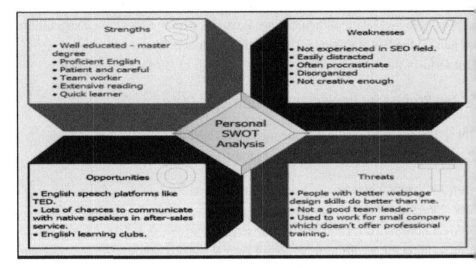

This is the second phase where we can assess and evaluate our abilities by Strengths we have in our personality, weakness we have, opportunity that surround us to perform the task and threats /risks that surround us which may impede our success.

Strengths and weaknesses are internal factors and opportunities and threats are external factors. A SWOT diagram analyzes these four factors and typically consists of four boxes, one for each area, but the exact shape may vary depending on the personality factors one has.

How to do a SWOT Analysis

- Determine the objective.

- Decide on a key project or strategy to analyze and place it at the top of the page.

- Create a grid.

- Draw a large square and then divide it into four smaller squares.

- Label each box. Write the word "Strengths" inside the top left box, "Weaknesses" inside the top right box, "Opportunities" within the bottom left box, and "Threats" inside the bottom right box. These are titles, so they should be distinguished from the rest of the text using either color or font size.

- Add strengths and weaknesses. Add factors that affect the project to the applicable boxes. Components of a SWOT analysis may be qualitative and anecdotal as well as quantitative and empirical in nature. Factors are typically listed in a bullet form.

- Draw conclusions. Analyze the finished SWOT diagram. Be sure to note if the positive outcomes outweigh the negative. If they do, it may be a good decision to carry out the objective. If they do not, adjustments may need to be made, or else the plan should simply be abandoned.

Step 3. Choosing your **Life's decision wisely**

Important Life choices to be made

- Get out of Comfort Zone
- Build Special Skills
- Using power of creativity and intelligence
- Choices to perform Smart Work vs Hard work

One leads a life based on Value system and a system of Beliefs. Many times in life, we are forced to choose between two or more options. It's not easy to make a decision, because everything you choose imprints on your life. It's easy to be overwhelmed in the moment and make a choice you regret.

"Everything In Life Is A Choice. Choose Wisely" T. Harv Eker

Life wouldn't be the same without choices - and who would want to give them up? -- but they can definitely make life tricky sometimes.

Throughout our lives we often find ourselves standing at the end of a road, wondering whether or not we should turn left or right. Sometimes we find ourselves on the same road we've been traveling down, yet we find ourselves yearning to take a turn down a different street.

The wonderful thing is that we have a choice. Unfortunately, the hardest thing is also the fact that we have a choice. So often we come to a place in our lives where we can decide whether we want something to stay the same or we want our lives to change, and it can be really difficult to make life-changing decisions.

Even more difficult can be the challenge of staying positive as you're struggling to determine what choice is best for you.

Your quest for personal excellence will depend upon various factors:

1. What you do – As an individual, you've got a leg up on most occupations as you directly contribute to your success.

2. How well you do it – If you are consistently performing to the satisfaction of others you will be appreciated.

3. The difficulty of replacing you – The better you are at something; the less likely it is that you'll be replaced by someone or something.

Step 4. Doing things differently- Create Your Niche/Excellence

Creating Your Exclusivity/Your Persona

- Doing unexpected things well
- Doing uncommon things
- Radiate by Sustained Individual Brilliance
- Create and Maintain your Niche

"Before you start some work, always ask yourself three questions – Why am I doing it, what the results might be and will I be successful. Only when you think deeply and find satisfactory answers to these questions, go ahead." Chanakya was a philosopher, economist, and statesman who wrote the Indian political treatise, the 'Arthashastra' (Economics).

In his quote, Chanakya gets at the heart of finding solutions to problems: you have to ask the right questions. His questions are great, because they're at the core of conversion rate optimization. If summarized, it is all about being able to justify ideas and create new ideas through sound justification.

To live a life of high achievement, you must fully believe in yourself and your abilities.

Find an extremely successful person who doesn't greatly believe in themselves. It's not going to happen. Steve Jobs, Martin Luther King, Jr., Michael Jordan, Elon Musk and Mark Cuban are just a few highly successful individuals who benefited greatly from this confidence. However, it's not their levels of success that we want to talk about. It's their willingness to get up again and again, when they failed or experienced a setback in pursuit of creating the life of their dreams.

They were only able to keep going and achieve success because of the level of belief in themselves, despite the enormous amount of failures they had experienced for years, leading up to their big breakthroughs.

Their dreams were big enough to take them eventually, where they wanted to go. Their belief is what created a vision so big, that they didn't care how many times they failed at something.

Step 5. Creating Center of Excellence – with Continuous Improvement

Center of Excellence (COE) lays solid foundation

- COE has Strategic Foundation
- COE helps in Review and Monitoring
- Continuous Improvement helps in Raising the Bar
- COE provides Leadership, Motivation & Success

Every structure must have a solid foundation if it is to be stable to withstand deterioration. The stronger a foundation the higher a structure can rise. While Continuous improvement takes you to greater heights, where once can achieve greater success and navigate with greater veracity and purpose.

Leaders do not command excellence, they build excellence.

Excellence is achieved by having an excellence character that engages in the entire leadership process.

A person with strong character shows drive, energy, determination, self-discipline, willpower, and nerve. They know what they want and are diligent in pursuing it. Conversely, a person with weak character shows none of these.

Foundations that support Excellence in Leadership

- **Convictions**. Every leader must have convictions. Rooted deeply within leaders are beliefs or convictions that are held onto steadfastly regarding people, concepts, life, death, religion, what is good, what is bad, what is human nature, etc.
- **Values**. These are attitudes about the worth of people, concepts, or things. The attitudes are lived out in actions. What you value will be reflected in your actions.
- **Skills**. The knowledge and abilities that a person gains throughout life. Abilities to learn a new skill varies with each individual. Some skills come almost naturally, while others come by study and practice.
- **Traits**. Character is the sum total of our traits. The more character traits displayed as a leader will result in others believing and trusting you.
- **Continuous Improvement** We need to continuously get better at what we do and achieve higher Excellences as no excellence is low enough or short enough for laying a strong foundation of Success.

Leader is successful as a person, someone who can Lead and motivate others.

Center of Excellence leads to an Individual's good understanding of his Personality, Positive Attitudes, and Belief in his abilities and Desire for Success.

"The will to win, the desire to succeed, the urge to reach your full potential...

These are the keys that will unlock the door

to your personal excellence"

—Confucius

Chapter 12

Steps for Implementing Corporate Center of Excellence

Business behaves differently in approaching the definition and values system, as this is not related to individual but collection of people and the goals is measured quantitatively or qualitatively as a strategic initiative of the organization.

Strategically a Center of Excellence (CoE) should, at a most basic level consist of: A team of people that promote collaboration and using the Best Practices around a specific focus area, in order to drive business outcome or customer-centric set of excellent result, on a continuous Improvement basis.

Why do we need Center of Excellence at Corporate Level?

The CoE concept begins by assembling a group of top experts in a specific business activity. This may be in a full-time role or as a specified percentage of their time because of their importance on other internal Business projects.

- The formation of these groups, one per expertise type, has great value from a productivity perspective.
- It saves multiple groups from continually "reinventing the wheel" by defining the same process again and again.
- The processes created by CoE are most likely more efficient than processes created on the fly by less qualified individuals.
- It facilitates process consistency, because everyone is following the same defined processes.
- A governing body exists to enhance the created processes and innovative ideas and process corrections are defined.
- Leverages combines the knowledge with this group in place. They leverage expertise to define best practices, create efficient processes, build formalized templates, construct appropriate checklists
- To write a group charter explaining how their expertise and created collateral can be used to benefit Business and the overall organization.

5 Steps for Implementing Corporate Center of Excellence

Step 1. Define the KPI: Strategic Vision

Step 2. Set up The SLA: Matrix of Performance

Step 3. Raise the Performance Bar: Quantitative vs Qualitative Trends

Step 4. Hit the Bull's Eye: Mitigate the Pain Points

Step 5. Set-up of Strategic COE Office -Under Commit vs Over Perform

Step 1: Define the KPI-The Strategic Vision

The key question asked is, "How well is a Business Organization performing, and to what extent Company is meeting success in its objectives?"

What is often missing from this evaluation, however, is the part about making sure that the employee is doing the right thing. After all, you may have a very hard-working and dedicated team member, but if he or she is not working on things that advance the organization's purpose, what is the point?

This is where **Key Performance Indicators(KPI)** come into play, and they apply both at the organizational and individual levels.

At an organizational level Key performance indicators (KPI) are a set of quantifiable measures that a company uses to gauge its performance over time These metrics are used to determine a company's progress in achieving its strategic and operational goals, and also to compare a company's finances and performance against other businesses within its industry.

KPIs also referred to as key success indicators or KSIs, they vary between companies and industries, depending on the strategic priorities or performance criteria. For example, if a software company's goal is to have the fastest growth in its industry, its main performance indicator may be the measure of revenue growth year over year (YOY). In the retail industry, store sales are a common metric used to measure sales growth between different store locations.

Some Examples of KPI's

KPIs are intrinsically linked to a firm's strategic goals and are used to help managers assess whether they're on target as they work towards those goals.

110

- A sales team might track new revenue, total revenue, new customer capture, average deal size, and deal pipeline size to assess progress toward corporate revenue targets.
- A customer support team might measure the average on-hold time for customers, as well as the percentage of calls that result in a high post-call survey rating and overall customer satisfaction.
- A marketing group will look at the contribution of marketing; generated sales leads to total revenue over time to gauge their effectiveness.
- Other areas of the business will look at the efficiency of processes and various quality metrics.
- Human resources will look at employee engagement, employee turnover, time-to-fill open positions and other related metrics.
- Managers and key stakeholders will monitor these indicators over time and adjust plans and programs as needed to improve the KPIs in support of the firm's strategic goals.

Step 2: Set up the SLA: The Matrix of Performance

The Service Level Agreement (SLA) is one of the most critical parts – if not the key element -- of IT Service Management (ITSM).

But as important as they are, they also can be complicated to set up. And some say they can be tricky to get right. However, when administrators do get them right, those SLAs not only help IT become more efficient, they enable IT to help the business. And that is the basic goal of IT Service Management (ITSM).

"A good agreement can do a lot. A good agreement will reduce outlays of capital and outlays for operations," says Rick Sturm, president of Enterprise Management Associates, Inc., a Boulder, Colo.-based IT research and analyst firm. "You can make it complicated, certainly, but it doesn't have to be. It shouldn't look like a Manhattan telephone book. It should be short and concise and cover a single service, and have a metric that covers user experience.

"But they don't make it easy for themselves, so there they sit," adds Sturm. "They could have these nice agreements that make their lives easier, but they don't."

An SLA is created when IT and business sit down and hammer out a contract -- this is what business can depend on receiving from IT, whether its availability, response time to a problem, or speed of service. It's also a tool for IT to show business executives exactly what the department can do. IT enables all of these business functions, and here is the paperwork that shows that they are living up to those obligations.

Service Level Agreements set the standards that IT needs to live by as they work as part of the overall business team. The most common use of SLAs is to ensure that incidents are resolved within a certain amount of time.

Service Level Agreement (SLA) is an agreement between two parties regarding a particular service. Apparently SLA must contain quantitative measurements that:

- Represent a desired and mutually agreed state of a service
- Provide additional boundaries of a service scope (in addition to the agreement itself)
- Describe agreed and guaranteed minimal service performance

SLAs vs KPIs

- Let us take a few examples that outline the differences. Consider a help desk service.
- SLA examples: Reaction time, resolution time, compliance to agreed deadlines etc.

- KPI examples (organization or service oriented): average reaction time for all customers, service desk employee load, incoming ticket volume trend, required capacity to fulfil SLA promises to customers

To sum it up – SLAs are about minimal, expected and agreed quality of a service provided to a customer; however KPIs are about desired operation efficiency and organization goals. It is important to measure both service level compliance and key performance indicators in order to keep promises and excel service quality. Both go together hand in hand.

How to Create a Strong Performance SLA

Defining the right metrics is only half of the battle. To be useful, the metrics must be set to reasonable, attainable performance levels. It should have parameters that have clear baselines.

Establish your Baseline

An SLA is only valuable if it's reasonably achievable. For example; while it's true that most site visitors will lose interest if a page fails to load within 3 seconds, setting 3 seconds as your SLA when most of your site pages currently take 8 seconds to load is unrealistic.

Benchmark against Competitors

Once you've established your own page performance baseline, the next step is to see how that baseline compares your competitors. While your goal might be to beat the page performance of your competitors, that may not be realistic for your initial SLA (again, performance goals and performance SLAs are different things). You can use your competitor's performance to help gauge what's reasonable.

Consider Key Questions

- At this point, you should have a good sense of the parameters for a strong initial SLA for your organization. It's a good idea to vet it by asking the following key questions:
- Which performance metrics do you want to include?
- What are acceptable thresholds for those metrics?
- What are your user's expectations?

Set up On-going Monitoring & Revisit SLA over time

Once you have your SLA outlined, vetted, and agreed upon, it's time to set up ongoing performance monitoring to ensure you don't violate it. As you continue to make performance improvements over time your frequency of meeting your SLA will tend towards 100%.

Step 3: Raise the Performance Bar: Engaging Workforce

You've most likely heard that the majority of the modern workforce is disengaged: *Gallup reports that only a meager 13 percent of the workforce is engaged*. There is a very good chance, then, that disengagement is currently harming your business and leading to suboptimal performance.

What's happening here is that an ineffective performance management system is in play, meaning that lower performers are allowed to happily coast along in blissful ignorance. They are clearing away the deck chairs while the boat sinks, so to speak. These deluded poor performers are never penalized, and they remain engaged in their jobs as a result. On the other hand, high performers are carrying the load — bailing water out of the sinking ship — and when they are not recognized for their efforts and contributions, they become disengaged.

To raise the standards of quality that are expected of or required for something, and since higher education became available to a greater number of people, businesses have increasingly been raising the bar for entry-level employees.

Organizations need very specific strategies to deal with the self-deluded cohort of happy low-performers.

The low Performers need to be encouraged and High Performers should become role models. There could be several ways

- Stretch Assignments "shape up or ship out" approach
- Employee Recognition Program
- Make people Responsible
- "Close" the Accountability loop
- Forge a Strong Link between Performance and Pay
- Assess and Reward Staff More Frequently

Step 4: Hit the Bull's Eye: Mitigate the Pain Points

"You can always find a distraction if you're looking for one" Tom Kite

As the ship sailed full speed ahead, little did they know that they were headed in the wrong direction. Ever feel like that? You're giving 110% but not getting anywhere? You've got no sense of direction and nothing to mark your small wins every day?

Pain points are simply tasks, habits, relationships or biases that are holding you back or causing you discomfort and stress.

Pain points are the things that cause us, well…. pain. These things are often easily mitigated and looked after through the cultivation of a few simple disciplines.

Certain Strategies and Systems help in Mitigating Pain Points

- Routines –Routines are a simple way to get rid of distraction. Like the distractions themselves, routines are replacing something with something else but this time replacing the worse with the better.
- Trainings- Employee training can help in gaining perspective for efficiency and skills, to get the job done better and more effectively.
- Discipline – Discipline helps to be productive quite easily. Although this one is much less sustainable, it can come in handy in times of difficulty. Routines allow us to go into auto-pilot.
- Positive constraints – i.e. committing to things that will stop you from doing other things. For example sending the weekly report by Thursday evening prevents failure not to submit on Friday morning.
- Gratitude – By being grateful, we don't have time for distractions. Make a routine of saying "thanks" helps in building a culture of positive human relationships and good manners.
- Vacation – Employees should be allowed to take timely vacations especially when they have stressed out during months of regular work behavior. Projects leading into another projects without gaps and time offs can lead to uncoherent worker and reduces efficiency.

Step 5: Making Outstanding things Happen, by Setting up Strategic COE Office in an Organization

Most organizations lack in setting up a Center of Excellence office as they have either not thought of it as strategy or as systems improvement. If they have a Top-Down approach; then the Senior Leadership deserves a blame for this, as Center of Excellence in not only an attitude issue, but also workmanship as to how someone wants to steer the ship.

When governance, a support structure, guidance, measurements and shared learning exists across an organization, the success is imminent.

Success will support organizational and specific projects goals. A need to gain results should be the primary motivation for creating any Center of Excellence. Or stated another way, the motivation/need for and expected results from a center of excellence should be well thought out, and articulated unambiguously to server as the foundation, for the creation of Center of Excellence. Without this, it cannot be successful.

Strategic centralizing the expertise in a COE has many positives

By definition, centralizing the expertise in a COE means, that expertise won't live under the multiple silos. Still, that's a small price for running a leaner, more nimble organization and eliminating potential duplicate efforts.

Consider that the benefits outweigh the downsides.

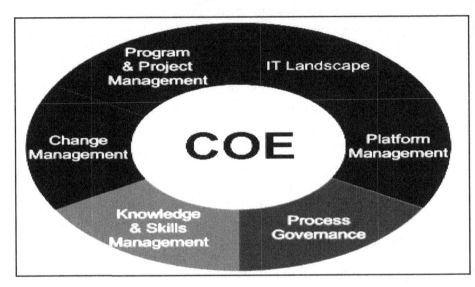

Center of Excellence is a Comprehensive and Holistic Framework which synergizes the entire Corporate Excellence:

- **Focus**: You get like minds working together, often resulting in a team that pushes each other's boundaries while focusing on the task at hand
- **Unified Commitment**: This speaks of organizational commitment across the board and not siloed to few and far between Business Units
- **Strategic Vision**: COE Office can be strategic office where uniform policy can be enforced among different businesses for a common corporate vision and singleness of purpose.
- **Economies of scale**: Better load balancing means you ultimately need fewer people to get more done.
- **Collaboration**: Your specialists are no longer laboring in isolation. The potential upside from peer-to-peer collaboration is limitless.

- **Quality**: You now can better enforce standards such as brand guidelines and style guides. Consistency across the organization saves time and fosters better quality output.
- **Training:** Providing training and oversight of the employees, especially when there are thousands of employees and multi-divisions with complex matrix settings.
- **Governing** the organization through appropriate resource allocation.
- **Single voice**: A single point of contact ensures consistency throughout the organization.

As companies scale in size, this organizational arrangement makes increasing sense, not only because it offers organizations the benefit of streamlined, creative, high-quality work, but also because this structure best supports the true customer journey—one that's dictated by the customer, at their own pace, not working in silos and taking different directions at their divisional levels.

By COE Business can establish a set of pragmatic principles guiding the management team, with strategic vision and sense of corporate direction.

Center of Excellence enables Organization to define a governance process for their best practices and standards and provides support in implementing them.

To be successful, time and technology demands that corporate leaders must choose Center of Excellence Framework, in guiding their ship dexterously on turbulent and unpredictable ocean currents of their business.

"Look at the sky - We are not alone.

The whole universe is friendly to us

And conspires only to give the best,

To those – who dream and work"

—A. P. J. Abdul Kalam

Conclusion

This book can transform an Ordinary person to an Extra-ordinary person.

Towering genius disdains a beaten path.

It seeks regions hitherto unexplored

(Abraham Lincoln)

The hidden potentials of our mind are more startling than the wonders of nature. There are marvelous achievements of human talents, intellectual and physical powers found in the world, which makes a person extraordinary.

THE KEY TAKE-AWAYS

Readers can gain a lot of common wisdom, which is uncommon.

In this book we have enumerated that as humans, we have amazing power in *Making Outstanding Things Happen* by making right choices, we can understand our Halo, our Personality traits and in combination with *Our Positive attitude*, **we can have an amazing Center of Excellence.**

We illustrated that we can have a systematic and organized process of knowing our abilities; knowing our Values & Beliefs, choosing our positive mindset for excellence, and constantly learning and improving the skills for performing the tasks, we can not only accomplish goals but also exceed expectations, and achieve *greater success in life* **to Make Outstanding Things Happen.**

A successful journey of the reader is envisioned into 3 simple steps:

Part One: Understand Your Halo: Values and Beliefs
Part Two: Take the Path: Make Outstanding Things Happen
Part Three: Implement Center of Excellence (COE) Roadmap

Part One: Understand your Halo: Values & Beliefs

- Chapter 1: What makes you tick -Personality Traits vs Personality Types
  - Allport classified 4,000+ Personality traits under 3 Cardinal categories
  - Factors that determine the Personality: 5 factors (OCEAN)
  - Preference of General Attitude Theory
  - 16 Personality types as per Myers-Briggs
  - What is your personality?: Take the personality assessment
  - How to Create Your Personality Chart on a 20-Point Personality Chart
  - We can Change our Personality, Understand our Temperament, Develop Leadership Character, and Build Excellence in Character
  - How to be an Effective Leader
  - Top 10 Traits of People with Leadership/High Excellences
- Chapter 2: Tap into your Powerful Sub-Conscious Mind
  - Realizing the Power of your Subconscious minds
  - Subconscious mind: Your Healthier Within
  - How to tap into your Subconscious mind: Follow 5 Simple Steps
  - Realize 10 Treasures of Your Sub-Conscious Mind
- Chapter 3: Use Amazing Powers of Creativity & Lateral Thinking
  - Definition of Creativity
  - The Process of Creativity: Developing your innovative prowess
  - The Logic of Creativity
  - Create Creativity Hit-list to "Generate Outcomes"
  - Improving Creativity: 5 Step Process
  - Definition of Lateral Thinking
  - Prudence of Lateral Thinking
  - 6 Hat Techniques
  - Lateral Thinking People are never short of Ideas
  - Synergy of Creativity and Lateral Thinking is a game changer
- Chapter 4: Attain Happiness: The 6 Keys
  - Why should we be happy?
  - On achieving Happiness: Creating Positive Center of Excellence
  - The 6 Keys to "Attain Happiness"
- Chapter 5: Treasure "12 Laws of Karma" that will change your life
  - Role of Karma in Center of Excellence of our life
  - 12 Laws of Karma

- Foundations that support Excellence in Leadership
- Chapter 12: Steps for Implementing Corporate Center of Excellence
  - 5 Step for Implementing Corporate COE
  - Strategic Centralizing expertise in a COE has many positives

This book brings a lot of good Learning, Inspiration, Motivation and nascent aura of delight to the readers.

A reader can develop his amazing potential by techniques, process and steps from this book and can learn a lot about his Abilities, Personality, Success factors, Creativity, Attitude, and develop Leadership skills etc.

All these Synergizes can lead to Make Outstanding Things Happen in his life.

This book showcases Roadmap to Implement the Path of Center of Excellence where a person can really Evolve and Transform his Persona, create a Niche fc himself/herself.

With our improved and amazing abilities, one can lead positively into his Dynamic and Successful Future.

"Success is no accident.

It is hard work, perseverance, learning, studying, and sacrifice

And most of all,

Love of what you are doing

Or learning to do"

—Pele

(World's greatest soccer legend)

About the Author

For the last 30+ years, Ajaya Gupta has contributed extensively with Motivational and Thought-Leadership in Editorial and Journalism arrays. In his early days, he launched First Management Journal for Institute of Management Technology during his MBA stint in 1981. As an Editor of "The Metropolitans" for Calcutta Jaycees, has won several State and National awards. Has authored 25+ Articles and Research papers, widely published in Tech Journals/Magazines.

His awesome inspirational and creative writings have brought motivation, learning and nascent aura of delight to the readers. Besides excellences with editorial and journalism awards, other recognition includes; Corporate Leadership and Excellence awards, Wall of Fame, International Who's Who, Awards for Creativity, Leadership and Outstanding Contributions.

His profile is rated Top 1% in the World @Linkedin-Pulse, where he has also contributed 11+ Articles, where one such Article "12 Laws of Karma that will Change Your Life" received 44,000+views and 1,000+shares, within few months.

He is Founder of "BPOP Group" for Best Practices in the Industry on Linkedin, where "Mind meets Excellence". The Group publishes over 100+ posting per year with News, Views, Articles, Adages, Thought Leadership and Industry Trends. The Group has now spread over to 27+ countries having several eminent Industry Leaders, Luminaries, Authors, Visionaries and International Elites.

Is highly innovative technology leader and visionary, travelled worldwide. Has a Techno-functional background rich with MBA, Engineering, ITIL, Six Sigma, Project Management, CISSP, Scrum Master, and Business Intelligence certifications. His passion of learning, teaching and imparting education has seen him as visiting faculty and guest speaker, at various professional institutions, seminars and management forums. He is on-board/distinguished panel member of several research institutions, technology panels and professional associations.

Currently based out of Los Angeles, USA, and for the last 8+ years has been Strategic IT Leader-Center of Excellence and Business Solutions /Director IT-PMO Projects, Global Operations with Fortune 100 IT Management Consulting Groups. Is also a Technical Advisor and Thought leader Making Outstanding Things Happen. Brings last 17+ years' experience in USA and prior 10+ years with International leadership, as Vice-President/Global Head/Technical Advisor based out of UK, India & SE Asia, with a history of outstanding success.

"The bird is powered by its own life and by its motivations. Sky is the limit."

Made in United States
North Haven, CT
27 September 2022

24643746R00085